**New Directions for
Community Colleges**

Arthur M. Cohen
EDITOR-IN-CHIEF

Caroline Q. Durdella
Nathan R. Durdella
ASSOCIATE EDITORS

Amy Fara Edwards
MANAGING EDITOR

Civic Learning and Democratic Engagement

Bernie Ronan
Carrie B. Kisker

EDITORS

Number 173 • Spring 2016
Jossey-Bass
San Francisco

CIVIC LEARNING AND DEMOCRATIC ENGAGEMENT
Bernie Ronan, Carrie B. Kisker (eds.)
New Directions for Community Colleges, no. 173

Arthur M. Cohen, Editor-in-Chief
Caroline Q. Durdella, Nathan R. Durdella, Associate Editors
Amy Fara Edwards, Managing Editor

NEW DIRECTIONS FOR COMMUNITY COLLEGES (ISSN 0194-3081, electronic ISSN 1536-0733) is part of The Jossey-Bass Higher and Adult Education Series and is published quarterly by Wiley Subscription Services, Inc., A Wiley Company, at Jossey-Bass, One Montgomery St., Ste. 1200, San Francisco, CA 94104. POSTMASTER: Send address changes to New Directions for Community Colleges, Jossey-Bass, One Montgomery St., Ste. 1200, San Francisco, CA 94104.

SUBSCRIPTIONS cost $89 for individuals in the U.S., Canada, and Mexico, and $113 in the rest of the world for print only; $89 in all regions for electronic only; $98 in the U.S., Canada, and Mexico for combined print and electronic; $122 for combined print and electronic in the rest of the world. Institutional print only subscriptions are $335 in the U.S., $375 in Canada and Mexico, and $409 in the rest of the world; electronic only subscriptions are $335 in all regions; combined print and electronic subscriptions are $402 in the U.S., $442 in Canada and Mexico, and $476 in the rest of the world.

Cover design: Wiley
Cover Images: © Lava 4 images | Shutterstock

EDITORIAL CORRESPONDENCE should be sent to the Editor-in-Chief, Arthur M. Cohen, at 1749 Mandeville Lane, Los Angeles, CA 90049. All manuscripts receive anonymous reviews by external referees.

New Directions for Community Colleges is indexed in CIJE: Current Index to Journals in Education (ERIC), Contents Pages in Education (T&F), Current Abstracts (EBSCO), Ed/Net (Simpson Communications), Education Index/Abstracts (H. W. Wilson), Educational Research Abstracts Online (T&F), ERIC Database (Education Resources Information Center), and Resources in Education (ERIC).

Microfilm copies of issues and articles are available in 16mm and 35mm, as well as microfiche in 105mm, through University Microfilms Inc., 300 North Zeeb Road, Ann Arbor, MI 48106-1346.

CONTENTS

INTRODUCTION

> The first and most essential charge upon higher education is that at all levels
> and in all its fields of specialization, it shall be the carrier of democratic values,
> ideals, and process.

As the preceding quote by President Truman's Commission on Higher Education report titled *Higher Education for American Democracy* (1947, p. 102) makes clear, concepts of civic learning and democratic engagement are central to the purpose of higher education. The Truman Commission thought this to be especially true for community colleges, institutions the commission promoted on a national scale in order to provide greater access to educational programs and services and to develop stronger communities. Indeed, as "Democracy's Colleges," or "The People's Colleges," community colleges perform (or, at least, were intended to perform) both a democratizing role—they facilitate social mobility by admitting all comers regardless of race, religion, socioeconomic status, educational preparedness, and professional or vocational goals, allowing more selective colleges and universities to admit some and turn away others—and a civic function: they engage students in preparing for life and work in their communities and in a democratic society. Ronan (2012) describes this duality in the community college mission as both "democratizing opportunity, and doing the work of democracy" (p. 31).

The democratizing role of American community colleges has received much attention in both the scholarly and popular literature, and numerous federal, state, and local programs have been put into place in order to increase access, provide targeted educational and support programs, and close achievement gaps among various community college populations. Historically, less attention—and far less support—has been given to the civic role of the colleges, although "our country urgently needs those attending these institutions—forty percent of all college students—to be informed and engaged citizens, skilled in democratic practices, knowledgeable about the policy issues their communities confront, and committed to lifelong engagement" (Kisker & Ronan, 2012, p. 2).

Nonetheless, two recent national reports have highlighted the crucial link between civic learning and the future of our democracy. The first, titled *A Crucible Moment,* emerged from a national task force aiming to take stock of how much progress colleges and universities have made in educating

NEW DIRECTIONS FOR COMMUNITY COLLEGES, no. 173, Spring 2016 © 2016 Wiley Periodicals, Inc.
Published online in Wiley Online Library (wileyonlinelibrary.com) • DOI: 10.1002/cc.20184

for civic learning and democratic engagement. Published by the American Association of Colleges and Universities' National Task Force on Civic Learning and Democratic Engagement in 2012, *A Crucible Moment* summarized this progress and made recommendations for making such learning more pervasive, integrated, and expected of every student. The second report, titled *Advancing Civic Learning and Engagement in Democracy* (U.S. Department of Education, 2012), outlined nine steps the U.S. Department of Education would undertake to advance the work called for in *A Crucible Moment*. Taken together, the reports provide a framework for the development of civic skills in the nation's institutions of higher education. They also acknowledge the necessary link between learning and engagement, between civic knowledge and active participation in the body politic.

Like these reports, this monograph uses the term *civic learning and democratic engagement* to encapsulate the variety of civic curricula, programs, practices, and opportunities for learning and engagement present on community college campuses. However, some chapter authors prefer *civic engagement*, the more common term in the national vocabulary. Unless otherwise specified, the terms can be used interchangeably; civic learning and democratic engagement suggests two dimensions, learning and action, which are often implicit in civic engagement.

It was to foster civic learning and democratic engagement for all community college students that The Democracy Commitment (TDC) was born in 2011. Pushing back against the contention that job training (despite all the national attention) is the sole mission of community colleges, TDC's goal was to create a national platform for community colleges to pursue civic work. A group of founding colleges helped to launch TDC and made a strategic decision to align with a similar national program among state colleges and universities, the American Democracy Project. This issue of *New Directions for Community Colleges* represents a collaboration among (some of) the colleges and partners active in TDC. The primary audience for this publication is the TDC network itself, as well as other community college faculty, staff, and administrators hoping to grow and enhance their institution's civic work.

Community college civic programs and practices take many forms. Although service learning continues as the modal civic activity on many campuses, the colleges have also been pursuing other forms of democratic engagement, including deliberative dialogues, community organizing and advocacy, Public Achievement and other civic agency programs, classroom discussion of policy issues, voter registration drives, candidate and election-issue forums, and opportunities to write or speak to legislators about issues of concern on campus or in students' communities.

Community college efforts to promote civic learning and democratic engagement are variously led by faculty, administrators, counselors, staff, and sometimes students. Some programs are highly institutionalized and supported on campus; others exist at the margins of the institution and are kept alive by a small group of true believers. At some colleges civic engagement is infused into the curriculum or embedded as a graduation requirement; elsewhere it exists primarily in extracurricular programming. Some colleges focus primarily on electoral politics and political engagement; others stress activism and involvement in causes dear to local communities. Approaches to endowing students with a sense of civic agency and the skills to participate in a democratic society are multiple and diverse, yet there is much similarity in the language used to describe the processes, and in the intended outcomes of each method.

As mentioned previously, service learning is the most common approach across the TDC network of colleges to engaging college students in local communities, and for many years it has helped students make meaningful connections between their coursework and the issues and challenges present beyond campus borders. However, the literature on service learning could fill its own volume of *New Directions for Community Colleges* and so we have decided to focus this issue on approaches to civic learning and democratic engagement that have received less attention in the literature and for which best practice examples and the lived experiences and advice of its proponents—immensely useful to college faculty and administrators—are less readily available.

Origins and Organization of the Volume

This volume of *New Directions for Community Colleges* originated in series of workshops convened by Derek Barker at the Kettering Foundation (in collaboration with the two of us) in which contributors to this monograph deliberated about civic learning and democratic engagement in community colleges, proposed and refined research questions, and shared the approaches their own campuses have taken to improve or enhance students' civic capacities. Chapters in this volume describe many of these approaches, along the way providing best practice examples and lessons learned from practitioners in the field. The monograph also attempts to place civic engagement into a broader philosophical framework and address some of the sticky issues with which civic practitioners and scholars are wrestling; for example: What skills do students need? What are the outcomes of civic learning programs and practices? How might civic competencies transfer to other settings? Is there a connection between civic skills and those valued in the workplace?

The volume is organized according to these purposes. After an introductory chapter by Carrie Kisker (Center for the Study of Community Colleges), which provides an overview of the types of civic programs and activities offered by TDC member colleges, the first few chapters provide a broader context for the concepts of civic learning and democratic engagement. Chapter Two, written by Bernie Ronan (Maricopa Community Colleges), explores the philosophical roots of civic learning and what skills are needed for students to become engaged in their communities and active in our democracy. Chapter Three, written by David Mathews (Kettering Foundation), discusses what it means to be meaningfully engaged in our society, why it matters, and how community colleges can assist in this work. In Chapter Four, John J. Theis (Lone Star College-Kingwood) describes the uncomfortable marriage between civic engagement and political science—the discipline it is most often relegated to—and calls for a reformulation of how we engage students in the wicked problems of democracy. Chapter Five, by Clifford Harbour (University of Wyoming), reports on a qualitative case study investigating the leadership qualities important to the development of civic engagement at a large, suburban community college.

The next several chapters are written primarily by community college faculty or administrators and explore specific ways in which colleges are engaging students in the work of democracy. Specifically, in Chapter Six Lavita McMath Turner describes the process of implementing a civic engagement graduation requirement at Kingsborough Community College, focusing in particular on how the college overcame several obstacles to implementation. Chapter Seven, written by Cynthia Kaufman (De Anza College), picks up where Chapter Five leaves off, further exploring faculty resistance to civic engagement and suggesting ways of conquering those fears in order to reclaim higher education's civic purpose. In Chapter Eight, Lisa Strahley (SUNY Broome) and Tracy D'Arpino (Johnson City Central Schools) describe a Public Achievement partnership between teacher education students and students at a local elementary school that led to all participants gaining a stronger sense of themselves as civic change agents in their communities. The final chapter in this section, written by Caryn McTighe Musil (Association of American Colleges and Universities), describes lessons learned from the *Bridging Cultures to Form a Nation* project, a collaboration among TDC colleges and the American Association of Colleges and Universities.

The volume then delves into some of the sticky issues mentioned previously, in particular questions related to the outcomes of civic programs and the transferability of those civic skills to other milieus. Chapter Ten, written by Kurt Hoffman, describes the civic cocurricular activities offered by Allegany College of Maryland, as well as the self-reported civic outcomes of its students. Hoffman points out that if Allegany—a small rural institution in the foothills of the Appalachian Mountains—can effect these outcomes, they may well be possible anywhere. In Chapter Eleven, Carrie Kisker, Mallory Newell (De Anza College), and Dayna Weintraub (University of California, Los Angeles) delve deeper into the ways in which community colleges can influence students' civic agency, behavior, and knowledge by reporting on the results of a civic outcomes survey piloted at four California community colleges.

Chapter Twelve, written by Jennifer Mair, describes Skyline College's student-centered approach to campus dialogue and deliberation and assesses the transferability of those skills to civic, workplace, and personal settings. And in the concluding chapter, Lena Jones takes the issue of skill transferability further by exploring the relationship between civic and workforce missions at Minneapolis Community and Technical College and by suggesting ways that they might be better integrated.

Taken together, these chapters provide readers with a sense of how community colleges are working to develop civic learning and democratic engagement on their campuses, as well as how they are dealing with the sticky issues that arise as part of this effort. It is our hope that the volume will both enrich the civic work occurring within the network of TDC schools and expose other college leaders, faculty, and staff to that work, thereby fostering more opportunities for institutions and their students to engage in their communities and in our democratic society in ways that are transformative for all involved.

Carrie B. Kisker
Bernie Ronan
Editors

References

Kisker, C. B., & Ronan, B. (2012). *Civic engagement in community colleges: Mission, institutionalization, and future prospects*. Dayton, OH: Kettering Foundation.

National Task Force on Civic Learning and Democratic Engagement. (2012). *A crucible moment: College learning & democracy's future*. Washington, DC: Association of American Colleges and Universities.

President's Commission on Higher Education. (1947). *Higher education for American democracy* (Vol. 1). New York: Harper and Brothers.

Ronan, B. (2012). Community colleges and the work of democracy. In *Connections: Educating for democracy* (p. 31). Dayton, OH: Kettering Foundation.

U.S. Department of Education. (2012). *Advancing civic learning and engagement in democracy: A road map and call to action*. Washington, DC: Author.

CARRIE B. KISKER *is an education research and policy consultant in Los Angeles, California, and a director of the Center for the Study of Community Colleges.*

BERNIE RONAN *is former associate vice chancellor for public affairs at the Maricopa County Community College District and cofounder of The Democracy Commitment.*

1

This chapter describes the ways in which civic learning and democratic engagement are incorporated into community colleges' missions and strategic plans, professional development, curricula, and extracurricular programming.

An Inventory of Civic Programs and Practices

Carrie B. Kisker

In 2012, roughly 60 community colleges across the United States—all members of The Democracy Commitment (TDC), a national initiative providing a platform for the development and expansion of civic engagement in community colleges—were asked to fill out a web-based inventory of the ways in which their college engages in civic programs, practices, and curricula. Survey questions focused in particular on each institution's intentionality or sense of purpose toward civic engagement, their level of academic and extracurricular focus on civic engagement, how civic engagement is assessed, and new program development. This chapter provides a top-line analysis of these civic inventories and is thus an illustration of the myriad ways in which TDC colleges are working to develop the civic capacities of their students. It should be noted, however, that the institutions referenced in this chapter do not represent all community colleges, and indeed their commitment to civic learning and democratic engagement is likely much stronger and more institutionalized than at schools that are not (yet) TDC signatories, possibly because many of the colleges surveyed are leveraging TDC to spur local civic efforts and initiatives. Nonetheless, this inventory provides us with a sense of the civic possibilities inherent in community colleges.

Institutional Intentionality Toward Civic Engagement

The first section of the civic inventory focused on institutional intentionality toward civic engagement; more specifically, whether and how community colleges incorporate civic learning or engagement in their missions, strategic plans, infrastructure, initiatives and programs, professional

NEW DIRECTIONS FOR COMMUNITY COLLEGES, no. 173, Spring 2016 © 2016 Wiley Periodicals, Inc.
Published online in Wiley Online Library (wileyonlinelibrary.com) • DOI: 10.1002/cc.20185

development, and so forth. Of all the institutions that filled out a civic inventory, the vast majority reported that civic engagement is either explicitly or implicitly mentioned in its mission statement, values, and/or strategic plan. For example, included in Valencia College's (Florida) mission, values, and strategic goals is "a commitment to institutional community involvement, community development, community service, civic leadership, civic engagement, and, of course, civic education." Allegany College of Maryland incorporates civic engagement into its philosophy statement: "We believe in democracy as a way of life, and in both the freedoms and responsibilities inherent in a democracy. We believe in preparation for active participation in a democracy." Other institutions, such as Broome Community College (New York) and Henry Ford Community College (Michigan) reinforce their commitment to civic work through their strategic plans. Wherever these statements appear, their incorporation into written values and strategic plans demonstrate that most of the responding colleges have made civic engagement a publicly stated priority.

Furthermore, most respondents reported that their institution has a campuswide civic engagement program or initiative focused on civic leadership and/or democracy building. For example, almost half of the colleges participate in regional or national civic organizations such as Campus Compact, a national coalition of schools committed to fulfilling the civic purposes of higher education; Public Achievement, a youth civic organizing model that helps students become agents of democratic change; or model United Nations programs, which provide students with a forum for addressing global concerns in a real-world context. In addition to these, most of the responding colleges reported offering locally grown programs geared toward civic engagement; these will be discussed later in this chapter.

Despite public commitments to civic learning and democratic engagement, less than half of the community colleges responding to the survey had an established center or office to guide these activities, and staffing and levels of support for these centers varied widely. The Center for Service-Learning at Mesa Community College (Arizona) and the Institute for Civic Engagement and Democracy at Miami Dade College (Florida), for example, both employ eight or more full-time staffers plus multiple student workers, America Reads Tutors, AmeriCorps VISTAs, and/or faculty liaisons and have annual budgets in the range of $350,000 to $500,000. Far more colleges with dedicated civic engagement centers employ one or two full- or part-time staff and use work-study students or grant-funded community organizers to fill in the gaps. At these centers, budgets are much lower, from $5,000 to $25,000 per year.

At community colleges that do not have dedicated civic engagement infrastructure, some carry out civic work through related centers (such as the Center for Student Involvement at Johnson County Community College in Kansas and the Office of Student Life and Leadership Development at

Lane Community College in Oregon). As well, several more have delegated civic work to faculty members or campuswide committees (Chapter Ten of this volume describes the success Allegany College of Maryland has had with this approach).

Another way to assess institutional intentionality toward civic engagement is to examine whether a college's faculty tenure or advancement program includes a civic engagement requirement or incentive, and if the college offers civically minded professional development opportunities for faculty and staff. Although only a handful of the responding colleges stated that their faculty tenure or advancement policies incorporate a civic requirement or incentive (Henry Ford, for example, requires all full-time faculty to contribute 20 hours of service per year within the institution's primary feeder communities), several others noted that such activities were considered informal expectations. And two-thirds reported existing professional development opportunities specifically focused on topics related to civic engagement, such as service learning and sustainability workshops; a "Building Citizen Professionals" conference (at Lone Star College-Kingwood, Texas); and paying for faculty and staff to attend annual TDC meetings.

Taken together, these details about community colleges' incorporation of civic engagement into mission statements and strategic plans, campuswide programs and initiatives, infrastructure, faculty requirements, and professional development suggest that—at these TDC colleges, at least—there is a high degree of intentionality around civic engagement. These institutions are committed, publicly and in writing, to the sense that students can and should be engaged in their communities and in the democratic process and that the college has a responsibility to help them in this endeavor.

Academic Focus on Civic Engagement

Part Two of the civic inventory focused on how and where civic engagement is incorporated into the academic functions of community colleges. Nearly half of the institutions completing the survey have a specific designation for civic engagement and/or service learning courses in the college catalog (the other institutions may have civically focused courses, but they do not have a special designation), and some also offer a certificate or degree in civic engagement or related programs. For example, Cuyahoga Community College ("Tri-C," Ohio) offers a certificate in conflict resolution and peace studies; the capstone course for this sequence incorporates a service learning component. Similarly, Delta College (Michigan) offers both a certificate and an associate of arts degree in global peace studies; Monroe Community College (New York) offers a degree in diversity and community studies; and Mesa offers a global citizenship certificate. Although Henry Ford does not have a collegewide graduation requirement, in 2011–12 it instituted a civic engagement requirement for all athletic teams. In 2013, Kingsborough Community College (New York) instituted a collegewide civic graduation requirement; its implementation process is described in Chapter Six of this volume.

Courses or programs focused on developing civic leadership are similarly well represented at these community colleges. Leadership opportunities for students include (among others) specific leadership courses or leadership development programs, certificates in leadership and social change (De Anza College, California), student governance opportunities, race- or ethnicity-driven leadership seminars, and civic leadership internships (Valencia College). Many of the responding institutions also offer formal service learning courses or programs; most assist their students in gaining internships in local businesses, community organizations, or public agencies or offices; and half incorporate civic engagement activities or requirements into their honors program (several more strongly recommend that honors students engage in the community in some meaningful way). Only a few of the colleges respondents reported offering programs or courses in community organizing or development.

In the most recent edition of *The American Community College*, Cohen, Brawer, and Kisker (2014) proposed the concept of integrative education—essentially a call for redefining the principles of general education to suit 21st century realities—and argued that that the bases for such a transformation already exist in the form of critical thinking, civic and democratic engagement, and sustainable development programs. Thinking along much the same lines, the civic inventory asked whether colleges also offer programs or courses in sustainability. The vast majority of the responding colleges offered at least one such course. Some, like Delta College, have approximately 30 courses with this designation, and others offer entire programs dedicated to sustainability. Examples include sustainability education and awareness programs for both faculty and students, a campuswide recycling program, and an annual alternative energy summit at Henry Ford; an alternative energy certificate program at Gulf Coast State College (Florida); certificate and associate degree programs in sustainability and ecological literacy and sustainable food systems at Mesa; and a Center for Sustainability at Moraine Valley College (Illinois). As well, Tri-C has a stated goal to "infuse sustainability literacy throughout the curriculum." Clearly, a dedication to sustainability exists side by side with these colleges' commitments to civic engagement.

Despite fairly consistent levels of intentionality toward civic engagement, there is substantial diversity in approaches to incorporating it into the academic or curricular functions of the college. Some institutions offer courses or programs in nearly all of the categories mentioned; others have chosen to focus on one or two areas, such as sustainability or service learning. There is no evidence that one model is more effective than another in engaging students in their communities or in our democracy; indeed the patterns of civic integration into academic programs likely result from a combination of varying institutional missions, available resources, and the backgrounds and passions of the faculty and administrators leading the civic initiatives.

Extracurricular Approaches to Civic Engagement

Just as there are a variety of approaches to incorporating civic engagement into community college academic functions, there are numerous ways of infusing civic work into the extracurriculum. However, one area of uniformity among the colleges is their involvement of student groups in civic efforts. Indeed, all of the colleges that filled out the civic inventory sponsor student clubs or organizations that undertake civic activities or events. And most of them reported that their student government engages in civic activities—at many institutions, this is a primary function of the organization. Estrella Mountain Community College (Arizona) strongly encourages student clubs to engage in civic participation, perhaps by volunteering at local hospitals, food banks, and other organizations or by sponsoring clothing, food, and hygiene drives for needy families. At Delta College, civic engagement is a requirement for all student clubs. Similarly, at roughly half of the responding colleges, campus newspapers engage specifically in civic activities or advocacy.

Although there is some consistency among survey respondents in terms of the ways in which extracurricular civic work is carried out (student government, clubs, and so forth), the *type* of civic activities in which students (and faculty, and staff) engage varies greatly. Many colleges hold candidate or election-issue forums; for example, Moraine Valley coordinated a "Meet State Senate Candidates" forum for the campus and wider community, Allegany College of Maryland did something similar for congressional candidates, and Johnson County's debate team hosted a mock presidential debate.

Other institutions hold forums on issues important to the student body or the wider community. For example, Glendale Community College (Arizona) presented a forum to address rising tuition costs and unemployment; Lane has a recurring visiting scholars forum on Islam; and the Community College of Allegheny County (Pennsylvania) offers a lecture series focused on regional topics, such as labor–management relations, energy, and transportation. Similarly, each year at Santa Fe College (Florida), professors in the social and behavioral sciences provide a series of talks about constitutional issues leading up to Constitution Day, and a separate annual event invites veterans from Iraq and Afghanistan to discuss their experiences in the wars. As well, Allegany College of Maryland has launched a series of campuswide events titled "Engaged Democracy: Ordinary People Making an Extraordinary Difference."

NEW DIRECTIONS FOR COMMUNITY COLLEGES • DOI: 10.1002/cc

In addition to forums, the civic inventories contained numerous other examples of extracurricular programs, awards, and activities leading to greater civic and democratic engagement. These include democracy walls (at Tri-C and other community colleges, these are mobile displays placed in various locations around campus intended to generate discussion and solicit responses to issues important to students and the community); National Day of Action activities (San Diego Community College District, California); workshops for high school students on community change and youth empowerment (De Anza); Constitution Week trivia games (Broome); Public Achievement (Delta, Lone Star-Kingwood); Martin Luther King Jr. Day of Service programs (Henry Ford); and deliberative dialogues, a form of discussion aimed at understanding others' perspectives and collaboratively finding the best course of action. (Chapter Twelve of this volume details dialogue facilitation training and outcomes among students at Skyline College in California.)

In addition to these civic efforts, the majority of responding colleges also engage in activities directly related to political and democratic processes. For example, nearly all colleges undertake voter education and/or registration activities; these drives are frequently organized or run by student government or other student groups in collaboration with faculty and administrators. Indeed, at some colleges, faculty offer extra credit to students who actively encourage or register family, friends, or community members to vote. Elsewhere, such as at Miami Dade and Moraine Valley, students are urged to sign up as poll workers, election judges, or voting equipment managers. During each year in which there is a presidential campaign, political student groups at Henry Ford coordinate teach-ins as a means of educating students about each candidate and the primary issues at stake in the election.

Miami Dade and other community colleges have also begun to work with TurboVote, which provides an easy, online way for students, faculty, and staff to register, request an absentee ballot, and/or receive email or text reminders on the days leading up to an election. Other colleges, such as Paradise Valley (Arizona), collaborate with Rock the Vote to host events promoting political participation on campus. Other common partnerships include the League of Women Voters, local county clerks' offices, and the Fair Elections Legal Network.

Clearly, the extracurriculum is an effective tool for developing civic capacity, and community colleges appear to be using it extensively in order to reach students whose chosen academic focus may not incorporate such skills or experiences. Furthermore, infusing a focus on civic engagement into the extracurriculum may be less political and potentially less expensive than incorporating it into the curriculum itself. Indeed, as Chapter Ten of this volume argues, it may allow community colleges to visibly and perhaps more easily make good on their public commitments to civic learning and democratic engagement.

NEW DIRECTIONS FOR COMMUNITY COLLEGES • DOI: 10.1002/cc

Assessment of Civic Engagement

One area of uniformity in the colleges' civic inventories was the lack of a comprehensive approach to assessing civic engagement. Almost all of the institutions participate in the Community College Survey of Student Engagement (CCSSE), but the CCSSE contains only one or two questions touching on civic skills or experiences. The Noel-Levitz Student Satisfaction Inventory—which one college reported using—similarly contains only one or two civic references. Community colleges are not the only institutions that lack a standardized instrument to assess civic engagement; the American Association of State Colleges and Universities and the Association of American Colleges and Universities recently collected instruments being used by colleges and universities to assess civic learning. The inventory they put together (Reason & Hemer, 2014) reinforces the dearth of instrumentation in this area.

Indeed, homegrown surveys created by institutional researchers and/or student evaluations of courses or extracurricular events are much more common ways of assessing civic engagement, if it is assessed at all (a few respondents indicated that they did not evaluate civic efforts in any way). In addition, some colleges directly or indirectly assess civic engagement as part of their accreditation process, although this depends on the accrediting body. For example, institutions reporting to the North Central Association's Higher Learning Commission use the Academic Quality Improvement Program (AQIP) to evaluate civic learning, and schools reporting to the Middle States Association of Colleges and Schools examine civic engagement as part of their institution's general education goal. However, several other accrediting bodies do not incorporate a specific focus on civic learning or democratic engagement, which means that for colleges in these regions, all assessment of civic programs or practices must be done at the local level. Regardless, it is clear that most community colleges could benefit from a common approach to assessing the outcomes of their civic efforts; Chapter Eleven of this volume details a new survey—currently in a pilot stage—that would do just that.

New Program Development and Goals for the Future

The last section of the civic inventory asked colleges about new civic programs or initiatives they planned to undertake, as well as their institution's goals surrounding civic learning and democratic engagement in the coming years. Many of the colleges listed programs they hoped to incorporate, including deliberative dialogues at Broome, a civic-focused Alternative Spring Break at Lone Star-Kingwood, and expanded opportunities for service learning at the Community College of Allegheny County.

Although none of the responding colleges used the term, institutionalizing a commitment to civic engagement was a common theme throughout their plans for the future. For example, Henry Ford planned to incorporate a Center for Civic Engagement, and Glendale was instituting a TDC working committee to "increase collaboration and communication with various units already emphasizing civic engagement." Allegany College of Maryland was hoping to unify their civic activities, making civic learning and democratic engagement an integral part of their institutional culture. Similarly, Delta College was working to incorporate civic engagement into its strategic plan and to create a civic engagement "umbrella" to coordinate all of the "activities surrounding civic engagement, service learning, and honors." Miami Dade noted that they planned to institute additional faculty workshops geared toward civic learning and democratic engagement "to help them make this part of how they teach." Gulf Coast State was incorporating civic and democratic engagement into its collegewide learning outcomes, and both Moraine Valley and Valencia colleges planned to develop courses and certificates in civic and democratic engagement. Santa Fe and Delta colleges both intended to engage in greater documentation and assessment of their civic efforts. By the time this chapter is published, many of these plans for the future will have already been accomplished and, ideally, civic learning and democratic engagement will have become further ingrained in the infrastructure and culture of each of these colleges.

What Can We Take Away from This Analysis?

Civic engagement tends to be defined and described broadly; even among TDC colleges, there is no consensus, and definitions range from the narrow (voting, being aware of the political process, service learning) to those encompassing broader themes of social justice, civic responsibility, and participation in a democratic society. Perhaps as a result, community colleges act on their civic intentions in a multitude of ways; some focus on curricular integration, whereas others use the extracurriculum as the primary tool for civic learning and democratic engagement. As such, although the civic inventories examined in this chapter do not move us any closer to a single definition, they do provide some insight into what civic engagement "looks like" at various community colleges across the nation.

The reasons behind these varied approaches to civic work are unclear; at some colleges, it may have to do with a lack of finances or infrastructure. At others, it may be because a single faculty or staff member has taken it upon himself or herself to civically engage students in the realm in which he or she has the most influence. Other patterns of civic programming may result from faculty resistance to curricular infusion or may simply be a reflection of a particular college's history and institutional priorities.

Although the community colleges highlighted in this analysis offer a diverse array of curricular and cocurricular civic programs, the one constant seems to be a public, written commitment to civic engagement. This intentionality is critical, as research suggests that it is a precursor to the institutionalization of civic programming. Yet for institutionalization to occur, these colleges—as well as other institutions around the country with similar commitments to civic learning and democratic engagement—will also need to recruit a wide swath of faculty and administrators to the cause; secure continuous, hard-money support for civic programs and initiatives; and further integrate civic ideas and practices into existing coursework and curricular programs (Kisker & Ronan, 2012). Based on the responding colleges' stated goals for the future and plans for expanding civic infrastructure and programming, it seems that many of the institutions included in this analysis are well on their way. This—along with the apparent high level of intentionality and the variety of approaches to developing students' civic capacities—is encouraging and, ideally, is an indication that civic learning and democratic engagement can truly become part of the mission and culture at our nation's community colleges.

References

Cohen, A. M., Brawer, F. B., & Kisker, C. B. (2014). *The American community college* (6th ed.). San Francisco: Jossey-Bass.

Kisker, C. B., & Ronan, B. (2012). *Civic engagement in community colleges: Mission, institutionalization, and future prospects.* Dayton, OH: Kettering Foundation.

Reason, R., & Hemer, K. (2014). *Civic learning assessment rubric DRAFT.* Washington, DC: Association of American Colleges and Universities and the American Association of State Colleges and Universities.

CARRIE B. KISKER is an education research and policy consultant in Los Angeles, California, and a director of the Center for the Study of Community Colleges.

2

This chapter looks at civic learning and democratic engagement from the perspective of political philosophy to suggest the essential cognitive, affective, and political skills needed for careers of fulfilling public work and for civic action.

Love of the World: Civic Skills for Jobs, Work, and Action

Bernie Ronan

Citizenship is the struggle, carried out through conversation, to achieve accounts of the world that accord with norms of friendship and provide grounds for action.

Danielle Allen

Students need skills to be democratically engaged citizens, and community colleges participating in The Democracy Commitment are working in myriad ways to develop and enhance these skills. But perhaps of greater importance to democracy is the attitude students have toward the world in which they will apply those skills. At one point, Hannah Arendt considered naming her masterwork on human activity *Amor Mundi* (love of the world), instead of what it was eventually titled, *The Human Condition* (Young-Bruehl, 1982). That alternate title offers a different perspective on the human activity analyzed in her book; it focuses on the world, rather than on the activities that affect the world (labor, work, and action). And, of course, the word "love" suggests the role of the heart as a political force.

The world that Arendt speaks of is not the physical world we inhabit with all its natural and artificial surroundings, though some human activity obviously touches on the physical world. She is speaking of the *polis* (Greek: city), the political world that humans shape; the "web of relationships" that they create through their speech and actions; and the space of appearance in which they organize themselves, appear to each other, and act publicly in pursuit of their common lives (Arendt, 2000, p.179). We are, as Aristotle

New Directions for Community Colleges, no. 173, Spring 2016 © 2016 Wiley Periodicals, Inc.
Published online in Wiley Online Library (wileyonlinelibrary.com) • DOI: 10.1002/cc.20186

23

said, *zoon politikon*, political animals (Everson, 1996, p. 13). It was the polis that Arendt wanted us to care about, and love.

The polis is not government, it is not the legislature, it is not elections, though these have come to seem coterminous in our parlance with the word "political." Laws that are made, how we govern ourselves, whom we select to do that governing, all these have an important relation to the polis, but they are not the world. The growth of the public sector and government has, in fact, denuded and crowded out the spaces in which humans can appear and act together. Re-creating these spaces is a main task of politics today.

The rarified atmosphere of legislative chambers may mimic in some fashion the type of polis that the ancients had in mind, but even in these settings, true deliberation rarely occurs. There are myriad other venues—town meetings, union halls, student clubs, even religious gatherings—in which the work of democracy is pursued today. Dubbed the "political wetlands" by David Matthews (2014), these informal spaces are where the modern polis can be found. And with the advent of modern information technology, the political world of relationships in which people interact and act on matters they deem important can be removed from physical space altogether and occur in the digital realm, which blurs even further what the polis means in our own time.

To address the skills that students need to operate in this changed political world, it is useful to start with the classic distinction between labor, work, and action that Arendt described in *The Human Condition*:

> All three activities and their corresponding conditions are intimately connected with the most general condition of human existence: birth and death, natality and mortality. Labor assures not only individual survival, but the life of the species. Work and its product, the human artifact, bestow a measure of permanence and durability upon the futility of mortal life and the fleeting character of human time. Action, in so far as it engages in founding and preserving political bodies, creates the condition for remembrance, that is, for history. Labor and work, as well as action, are also rooted in natality in so far as they have the task to provide and preserve the world for, to foresee and reckon with, the constant influx of newcomers who are born into the world as strangers. However, of the three, action has the closest connection with the human condition of natality; the new beginning inherent in birth can make itself felt in the world only because the newcomer possesses the capacity of beginning something anew, that is, of acting. In this sense of initiative, an element of action, and therefore of natality, is inherent in all human activities. Moreover, since action is the political activity par excellence, natality, and not mortality, may be the central category of political, as distinguished from metaphysical, thought. (Arendt, 1958, pp. 8–9)

Our focus is not on the controversies associated with Arendt's notion of labor or her distinction between work and political action. She was revisiting ancient distinctions between the realm of menial labor, with its drudgery; the realm of fabrication, where things are made for the world (which she called work); and the most important realm, that of action, where citizens act together to do something new in the world. Although the connotations of labor, work, and action have changed over the years, the three categories offer useful guides to thinking about political activity and the skills students need to engage in it. And though *The Human Condition* was an analysis of human activity, it was above all a clarion call, resounding a half century later, for us to rescue politics (read: action) from the dire threats it faces in contemporary societies.

Labor and Work

The alienation of labor that Marx first posited, and that Arendt analyzed in the context of the 20th century working world, continues apace in the 21st century. Jobs might now be seen in many cases as the analog of her term "labor," activity that serves biological necessity and survival and is often characterized by drudgery. Even Information Age jobs and many public sector jobs have this quality. Whereas labor was needed for survival, Arendt characterized work by the creation of artifacts, objects whose permanence affected both the physical and political worlds. Her characterization of work now seems almost anachronistic—the carpenter in his workshop; this was not meant to denigrate work but to accentuate action.

Although work in the Information Age likewise generates artifacts, these are literally ethereal and fast changing. Just as labor has changed in the past half century, mainly by fostering greater world alienation, so too our connotations for "work" have shifted. Work, as opposed to one's job, has come to have a vocational quality in some cases. As one community college professor often tells her students, "My job is not my work" (L. Jones, personal communication, September 30, 2014). Whereas one does one's job to "make a living," one's work may or may not find its way into one's daily occupation, but it gives one's life a sense of purpose. What typifies this new meaning of work is the notion of a vocation, a calling that comes from the political world to do something to build up the world and enhance it, a sense that one was meant to do this one particular work in one's life (Coles & Scarnati, 2014).

This understanding of work speaks of purpose, a reason for doing something in the polis that is worldly, public, civic. This purpose bestows on the work its political significance, its meaning. Kayla Mueller, the humanitarian worker killed by ISIS in 2015, moved from job to job, but what was constant was her *work*—her advocacy and her action. A colleague described her as having "an amazing clarity of purpose" (McKinnon, 2015, n.p.). Mueller was truly a citizen. If civic work is sustained over a lifetime, it can become one's "body of work," a lasting legacy of good done for the world. Because its purpose is the care the worker or laborer feels for the world, and the need one feels to show that care, this kind of activity instantiates what Arendt called *amor mundi*. As Robert Frost (1958) lyrically put it: "Only where love and need are one / And the work is play for mortal stakes, / Is the deed ever really done / For Heaven and the future's sakes" (pp. 238–240).

Whereas Arendt argued that labor and work are prepolitical activities, because they do not affect action in the polis, the world has changed so dramatically that one could now argue that the job that one does, however laborious and menial, as well as the work that one pursues as a vocation, do affect the political world. With the rise of what Arendt called the *social*—the growth of market capitalism, the rise of consumerism, the blurring of public and private—politics and the realm of the political (by which we do not mean electoral politics) now pervade virtually all aspects of modern life (Passerin d'Entreves, 2014). This means that a job working on sustainable energy, humanitarian service such as that done by Kayla Mueller, or other occupations or endeavors that affect the politics of how we live together in the material and digital worlds, all these can be seen as connected to and influencing the polis, the web of relationships in which we live.

Participation in such human activity that affects the world is a moral issue (Elshtain, 2013) because it implies that the one doing the activity sees it as good—when it is perceived as good for the target of the activity, it then becomes good for the agent (Sokolowski, 1992). And as these laborers and workers do good because they know and see it as good, they build up the habit of doing so. As Alexis de Tocqueville said in *Democracy in America* (1969), "By dint of working for the good of one's fellow citizens, the habit and the taste for serving them are at length acquired" (pp. 512–513). The benefit to the doer redoubles because the purpose of life is not only to address the issues posed by life in the polis and seek to better things, it is also to flourish, to be happy; and when one has a purpose in life, one flourishes (Keyes, 2012).

Action

Although having a job that enriches the world or pursuing a life's work or vocation to better the human condition is noble and worthwhile, action is the preeminent political activity. Done individually or collectively, human action "creases the world," it is something done toward and before others that changes the situation in which one finds oneself, that alters this web of relationships, that literally changes the world (Sokolowski, 2008, p. 257). To an extent that is not true in jobs or in work, action is inevitably tied up with speech; the two are usually found together. Speech can be a form of action, and we reveal ourselves as agents in a unique fashion when we act and make a difference in the world, first through deeds and then through words

(Arendt, 1958). Through speech we explain our actions, and actions often validate the integrity of what someone is saying. Plurality defines action. When we act, we act into a world with others, whether we act individually or together, whether the action occurs in a fourth-grade classroom where students are doing Public Achievement or in Tahrir Square during the Arab Spring. To restore politics, our goal must be to foster more opportunities for civic action.

Action also has the unique ability to reveal who we are, as agents, rather than what we are, as persons. Because action implies a world of others, and relies on the individual initiative of the actor or the initiative of a group working in concert (both of which are infinitely complex and impossible to forecast), action has a unique revelatory quality, especially when accompanied by speech, an ability to show us to the world for who we uniquely are (Canovan, 1974). Although doing a job each day does somehow define us (The frequent conversation starter: "What do you do?"), it does not reveal us in the unique way that action does. This is why Arendt cites natality—the fact that humans are born and therefore have an utterly distinctive ability to do the new, that is so characteristic of action. In fact, as Arendt (1958) points out, the Greek word for begin (*archein*) is similar to the Latin word *agere*, to act or to set something in motion.

Humans create these "spaces of appearance" in order to literally have room in which to speak and act together. And it is collective action that in fact sustains the space, the world, and continues it in existence. As long as people who have come together to collectively undertake some common purpose continue to deliberate about the best course of action and sustain their civic relationships with each other through such action, the space can be continually created and maintained (Passerin d'Entreves, 2014). What those who act together in this public way discover through their actions, the very capacity to act for this political purpose that has brought them together, is what Arendt (1958) called power. Unlike strength or force, power is the capacity to act in concert, and it gains its legitimacy from the people undertaking their collective action, not from some outside source that bestows it upon them. This power appears in public, which means two closely related things: that what the actors do together can be seen and heard by everyone and that it is something they share in common, rather than some private possession.

Community Colleges and Instilling a Love of the World

How does Arendt's conception of action relate to the civic initiatives we undertake at community colleges and other institutions of higher education? Elinor Ostrom, who won the Nobel prize for her life's work addressing how people solve collective action problems, said this about civic skills: "When de Tocqueville discussed the 'art and science of association,' he was referring to the crafts learned by those who had solved ways of engaging in collective action to achieve a joint benefit. Some aspects of the science of association are both counterintuitive and counter-intentional, and thus must be taught to each generation as part of the culture of a democratic citizenry" (Crittenden &Levine, 2013, n.p.).

Levine (2013)—defining civic engagement in a more robust fashion than is normally the case with this term—sees it as having three components: fostering deliberation, attending to civic relationships, and undertaking collaborative work and action. These three dimensions bespeak skill development occurring along a "spectrum" in each dimension, which involve intellectual, emotional, and political skills: the head, the heart, and the hands (Ronan, 2011). These skills, which the ancients called *virtues*, can be inculcated and fostered at some level, whenever humans choose to convene and sustain a polis—whether in a social club or a church meeting, a union hall or a classroom discussion.

The Head.   The intellectual or cognitive skill in this civic spectrum is practical reason, *phronesis* in Greek: judgment, prudence, or what could be termed savvy (the head). Phronesis is not theoretical knowledge, it is focused on action, on getting something done in the world (Aristotle, 1925). This savvy is acquired principally through deliberation, which revolves around how to take the practical steps in order to function as a "city." People learn from the experience of interacting with each other. They learn the art and practice of dialogue: the tools and concepts they need to produce practical, actionable conclusions and how people in community define and talk about their problems in order to act together. Through their deliberations they generate "public knowledge," knowledge about the world and how to act in it that they discover through the give and take of deliberation over time. This civic skill is experiential: students acquire it by deliberating and working together on some common issue.

The Heart.   The affective or emotional skill or virtue is civic friendship (the heart). The shared aspect of public knowledge that appears in a polis through deliberation and shared action forges a bond among the participants, a special civic relationship. They become *civic friends*. This *civic friendship*, in one of Aristotle's (1925) most startling statements, is what holds cities together. This special relationship among citizens acting in concert is a public thing, unlike the personal friendships that people enter into in their private lives. It is evident in feelings of solidarity the participants share for the import of the work, reflected in how they look out for and support others engaged in their work as if they were *second selves* (Aristotle, 1925), and illustrated in the common project of creating and sustaining the life of the city. Such civic friendship is mutual benevolence, mutually recognized (Sokolowski, 2008). As another political philosopher, Danielle Allen (2004), says: "Aristotle's biggest philosophical claim about politics is that our political relationships with fellow citizens are no different than friendships" (p. 137). Arguably, the notion that civic education entails matters of the heart seems foreign to us, yet any substantive reflection on our own experience of civic action, or that of others, will quickly reveal that the heart is involved, that civic relationships do matter greatly for the ultimate success of any public work or action. Students must be schooled in the salience of civic friendship if civic work and action are to gain greater traction in our world.

The Hands.   The political skill requisite for rejuvenating a love of the world in our common life is empowered action (the hands). This civic power is self-reinforcing as long as citizens continue to deliberate, giving them a sense of efficacy, a sense of agency. Citizens in these civic experiences come to have a sense that their words and deeds matter, that what they are doing has significance. In contrast to other human activities, collective action is the consummate political activity, and students must be given regular opportunities, in school and in their communities, to engage in collective action and to learn from the results, growing in the savvy they need to act in the world and in appreciation of the civic friendships they build through acting together.

Fostering the growth of jobs that have a civic purpose is important, as is recalibrating existing jobs so they have a more civic intent, a more purposeful direction to affecting the world. One could begin with the millions of public sector jobs in this country, so many of which focus on bureaucratic intent rather than empowering the job holder to engage the political world with their head, heart, and hands. Although such public sector jobs are arguably civic in legislative intent, they are nonetheless often typified by mindless drudgery rather than engagement with citizens, thus the term "bureaucratic." Although it is ironic that we even need to discuss the public value of public sector jobs, it is encouraging that the government sector, at least at the level of public administration theory, is actively discussing the notion of *public value* in public sector jobs (Bryson, Crosby, & Bloomberg, 2014), calling for more democracy in public work, promoting dialogue and deliberation and active collaboration with citizens. It is also encouraging that the private sector and the nonprofit sector are developing jobs that have an avowed civic intent.

Of greater import for the sake of our political life is the encouragement of students to confront the polis, with all of its conflicts and challenges, and to answer the call to civic work to care for the polis, to crease the world with actions that benefit the world and enable the student to flourish. This kind of civic work can be pursued outside the confines of the job one undertakes due to economic survival, and it can be undertaken through volunteer activities with others, through digital convenings in social media to advocate for a common cause, through faith-based endeavors that address human suffering, and so forth. Finally, students must be encouraged to undertake collective action, to enter the fray of a polis that matters to them and engages their interest, to deliberate with their fellows about whatever cause or interest has brought that space of appearance into being in the first place, to discover in their interlocutors new civic friends who share their common interests and support their work, and to roll up their sleeves and act in the world. This is the purpose for which we were all born into the polis, which was there before we came and will last beyond our leaving.

References

Allen, D. S. (2004). *Talking to strangers: Anxieties of citizenship since Brown v. Board of Education.* Chicago: University of Chicago Press.

Arendt, H. (1958). *The human condition.* Chicago: University of Chicago Press.

Arendt, H. (2000). Labor, work, action. In P. Baehr (Ed.), *The portable Hannah Arendt* (pp. 167–181). New York, NY: Penguin Books.

Aristotle. (1925). *The Nicomachean ethics* (D. Ross., Trans.). Oxford, UK: Oxford University Press.

Canovan, M. (1974). *The political thought of Hannah Arendt.* New York: Harcourt Brace Jovanovich.

Bryson, J. M., Crosby, B. C., & Bloomberg, L. (2014). Public value governance: Moving beyond traditional public administration and the new public management. *Public Administration Review, 74*(4), 445–456.

Coles, R., & Scarnati, B. (2014). Beyond enclosure: Pedagogy for a democratic commonwealth. In D. W. Brown & D. Witte (Eds.), *Higher Education Exchange, 2014,* 65–79.

Crittenden, J., & Levine, P. (2013). Civic education. In E. N. Zalta (Ed.), *Stanford encyclopedia of philosophy.* Retrieved from: http://plato.stanford.edu/entries/civic-education/#CosEdu.

de Tocqueville, A. (1969). *Democracy in America* (G. Lawrence, Trans., J. P. Mayer, Ed.). Garden City, NY: Anchor Books.

Elshtain, J. B. (2013). The moral imperatives of civic life. In D. W. Harward (Ed.), *Civic values, civic practices* (pp. 47–56). Washington, DC: Bringing Theory to Practice.

Everson, S. (Ed). (1996). *Aristotle: The politics and the constitution of Athens.* Cambridge, UK: Cambridge University Press.

Frost, R. (1958). Two tramps in mud time. In O. Williams (Ed.), *A pocket book of modern verse* (pp. 238–240). New York: Washington Square Press.

Keyes, C. (2012). The eudaemonic and the civic. In D. Harward (Ed.), *Civic provocations* (pp. 19–24). Washington, DC: Bringing Theory to Practice.

Levine, P. (2013). *We are the ones we have been waiting for—The promise of civic renewal in America.* Oxford, UK: Oxford University Press.

Matthews, D. (2014). *The ecology of democracy: Finding ways to have a stronger hand in shaping the future.* Dayton, OH: Kettering Foundation Press.

McKinnon, S. (2015, February 11). Mueller took global journey steered by those in need. *The Arizona Republic.* Retrieved from http://www.azcentral.com/story/news/local/arizona/2015/02/11/kayla-mueller-global-journey-steered-need/23219947/.

Passerin d'Entreves, M. (2014). Hannah Arendt. In E. N. Zalta (Ed.), *Stanford encyclopedia of philosophy.* Palo Alto, CA: Stanford University, Center for the Study of Language and Information. Retrieved from http://plato.stanford.edu/entries/arendt/.

Ronan, B. (2011). *The civic spectrum: How students become engaged citizens.* Dayton, OH: Kettering Foundation.

Sokolowski, R. (1992). What is moral action? In *Pictures, quotations and distinctions* (pp. 261–276). Notre Dame, IN: University of Notre Dame Press.

Sokolowski, R. (2008). *Phenomenology of the human person.* Cambridge, UK: Cambridge University Press.

Young-Bruehl, E. (1982). *Hannah Arendt—For love of the world.* New Haven, CT: Yale University Press.

BERNIE RONAN *is former associate vice chancellor for government affairs at the Maricopa Community Colleges and a cofounder of The Democracy Commitment.*

3

This chapter examines how the work of community colleges relates to the democratic work that citizens must do and makes the case for better alignment between the two.

The Community College's Role in Helping to Make Democracy Work as It Should

David Mathews

I am writing this chapter from within a research foundation—Kettering— that studies democracy from the perspective of citizens and communities. I realize that I am an outsider looking in when it comes to community colleges. But these colleges seem even more crucial to me at a time when citizens feel pushed to the sidelines by a political system in which they have little confidence—and at a time when their communities struggle to come together to combat persistent, deeply entrenched problems.

How are colleges and universities responding to these issues? Certainly higher education is awash in civic engagement and service initiatives. That's good. However, the community colleges that have joined The Democracy Commitment (TDC) are raising the bar by adding the word "democracy" to describe what they hope to do. This commitment may take these colleges beyond the good work of providing useful knowledge and other services to their communities.

What direction the TDC will take depends on how the colleges in it understand democracy. For a great many institutions, democracy means representative governments created by contested elections. For others, it has little precise meaning; it is no more than "the way life ought to be." That was implied in the response one university president gave when asked how her institution served democracy. We serve, she said, just by existing. There are, however, more demanding definitions, such as that in Ben Barber's (2003) writing about *strong democracy*.

At the Kettering Foundation, we think of strong democracy as a political system in which people have the power to shape their future. This definition is inherent in the word "democracy" itself, which has two roots: *demos*, which refers to the people collectively, and *cracy* (from *kratos*),

New Directions for Community Colleges, no. 173, Spring 2016 © 2016 Wiley Periodicals, Inc.
Published online in Wiley Online Library (wileyonlinelibrary.com) • DOI: 10.1002/cc.20187

which refers to their power. Power is the ability to act, so it would seem to follow that a democratic citizenry must act; it can't be a passive body. Citizens have to be more than informed recipients of services and more than voters. One way the citizenry acts is by doing the work required to produce the public goods that serve the common good. These range from local initiatives such as coming together to build a park for children to creating a national campaign to get drunk drivers off roads.

Following this line of reasoning, if community colleges see citizens as producers, they must be committed to doing their work in ways that align with or reinforce the work these citizen producers do. And for this alignment to occur, colleges need to understand how citizens work. Kettering has spent decades trying to better understand this. This chapter draws on our larger body of research and on multiple publications that report on how institutions of all kinds might better align their work with that of citizens. Alignment isn't as easy as it might appear because the way citizens do civic work is different from the way institutions of higher education do their work.

Troubled People, Troubled Communities

Why try to align these two ways of working? Is it just a matter of political philosophy? No, it is more than an abstract issue these days. Americans are anxious about what lies ahead for the country. Not only has confidence in government hit a record low, but people are also critical of most other major institutions, including those in education. Citizens feel they should step in and make a difference, yet they aren't sure how. Communities can overcome some problems with effective leadership and strong institutions. Yet other problems have a great many causes; there isn't one solution that will eliminate all of them. And these problems keep coming back. They defy even our most expert experts and have no technical solutions. Such especially persistent problems have been called *wicked*. An example is the hard-core poverty that persists in the face of prosperity.

When faced with wicked problems, people are troubled by the discrepancy between what is happening to them and what they think *should* be happening. But they don't agree on what the problems are, much less what should be done about them. And the disputes aren't over questions of fact but over what is the *right* thing to do. Citizens have to judge that for themselves; there aren't any experts on what is right. The ability of citizens to exercise sound judgment in the face of disagreements and uncertainty is critical to the work they do.

Starting Locally

I believe community colleges have an inherent advantage in addressing the concerns of citizens and the wicked problems of communities. These

NEW DIRECTIONS FOR COMMUNITY COLLEGES • DOI: 10.1002/cc

colleges aren't just physically located in communities. They are *of* their communities; they are integral to them. Quintessentially local in character, they reflect a particular way of life rich in its distinctive culture. That doesn't make the colleges parochial; many have an international constituency. But their close relationship with their communities gives them direct contact with people who experience democracy first hand and personally through local organizations and civic initiatives.

This direct contact can help community colleges avoid misalignment with the work of citizens, which can undermine a college's well-intended efforts to serve its community. That mismatch has sometimes been obvious when colleges and universities have tried to help communities hit by disasters. Take the case of hurricanes and tornadoes. When they strike, citizens themselves must act because survival depends on it. After a tornado has touched down, for example, it is often the case that no outside assistance can reach residents quickly because roads and power lines are gone. People live or die depending on their ability to come together to do the work of rescuing victims. Even when human-made disasters such as economic reversals have occurred and a revival is slow in coming, communities that are resilient have benefited from the ability of people to work together to recapture a spirit of enterprise and innovation.

When any kind of disaster strikes, institutions of higher education can and do provide valuable technical assistance and armies of volunteers. Still, although helpful, these responses don't speak to the most challenging question people ask, which is, "What can *we* do ourselves?" not, "What assistance can someone bring?" Citizens have to come together as a community in order to restore their community.

Colleges and universities have had difficulty responding to this question because the answer requires more than service and expertise. Yet they must respond, which is why they have to better align their work with the work citizens must do to rebuild communities. So recognizing the differences between these two types of work is crucial, despite the difficulties.

The Way Citizens Work

The Kettering Foundation has spent more than 3 decades trying to understand how citizens go about their work. Although we haven't learned all we need to know, I can tell you what we've found so far.

Like any kind of work, the work of citizens is made up of certain practices. All of them go on simultaneously, yet they are distinct. And they aren't techniques or steps in a progression; rather, they are truly practices, which aren't the same. I emphasize this distinction because techniques for facilitating meetings and planning are so widely used that the distinctiveness of practices is easily lost. I also stress this difference because techniques can bring with them an interventionist politics of "operating" that tries to fix others rather than build on inherent capabilities.

New Directions for Community Colleges • DOI: 10.1002/cc

Techniques have a specific task to accomplish. For instance, hammering is a carpenter's technique; its only benefit is driving a nail or shaping metal. And it is an acquired skill. The practices that citizens use are different; they draw on innate capacities and have intrinsic value. They are fulfilling rather than just utilitarian means to specific ends. Singing together is an example of a practice. The value is music, not just sound.

The work of citizens is done through practices, and Kettering research has identified six of them so far. These practices are democratic in that their value comes from increasing the control that people have over their future. Here are some of the six and how they differ from the way institutions work. The other practices are described in the latest Kettering report, *The Ecology of Democracy* (Mathews, 2014).

Naming Problems and Framing Issues. All work requires identifying what needs to be done or *naming* the problem to be solved. Academic institutions typically rely on professionals, who naturally describe problems in expert terms. Citizens, on the other hand, tend to see problems in terms of what is most valuable to them. Professionals' names are perfect for what they do, yet their solutions usually offer little role for citizens as producers.

When I say "valuable," I don't mean "values." I mean the *things that are critically important* to our collective well-being. These are intrinsic and shared. Most of us want to be secure from danger, to be free to act, to be treated fairly by others. These imperatives are similar to the individual needs psychologist Abraham Maslow found common to all human beings, such as the need for food, water, and shelter. People don't have to use special techniques to uncover what is deeply valuable to them; they can talk readily about how problems affect them and their families.

The difficulty when people try to work together isn't that they don't care about the same things; it is that their circumstances differ, which means they have different priorities. Recognizing that people share the same concerns but face different conditions can make relationships less adversarial, which promotes working together.

A related activity to naming problems is laying out the different options for carrying out what needs to be done. The options people will consider are based on what they feel is valuable or want to protect. And because they hold many things dear, they have numerous options to consider for combating a problem. There are also tensions among and within each option; that is, there are drawbacks to consider.

An option that serves one purpose well may not suit another objective. And every option has advantages and disadvantages, so there are costs and consequences to reckon with. When people have an opportunity to put all the major options they want to consider on the table, with their pros and cons fairly presented, they create a framework for sound decision making. This is different from the usual framework that consists of options that are polar opposites. And yet the broader framework still exposes the tensions that have to be worked through in any decision. Unless this happens, unrecognizable tensions tend to reemerge and interfere with work that citizens must do.

Professionals create frameworks for decision making as well, although the options are typically based on technical feasibility and the weight of scientific evidence. And they use techniques such as cost-benefit analysis to select options. These frameworks, however, may not include the options citizens want to consider. When that happens, there is serious misalignment.

Making Decisions.   No work can be done collaboratively unless those who need to work together decide on what the work should be—together. As they should, professionals tend to rely on hard evidence and their powers of reason to make decisions. Although citizens shouldn't ignore evidence, they rely on their innate faculty for judgment to determine what is the right thing to do. Citizens make judgments by deliberating. That is, they weigh possible courses of action against the various things they hold dear. Although human beings have the ability to make sound judgments, they may not use it well or at all. Still, it's a practice that is available.

Professionals often try to educate the public with facts, only to be frustrated by what they perceive as either ignorance or indifference. Citizens may try to engage professionals in what they hope will be a shared struggle over issues of what *should* be done, only to be met with more facts. The misalignment can be extreme.

Learning as a Community.   After the work is finished, both institutions and citizens reflect on what they've done to determine whether what they wanted to accomplish actually happened. The difference is that most institutions evaluate their efforts by comparing results to fixed goals. They measure. In the best cases, citizens and their communities learn by reassessing what they thought to be most valuable as well as reassessing the results of their collective efforts. They *reevaluate*.

Institutions seldom have the latitude to fail, but communities can fail successfully if they learn from their mistakes. Community learning is not a separate practice but rather something that can occur throughout the work of citizens. It provides the momentum to keep the work moving ahead on the most wicked of problems.

The question is how institutional or professional assessments relate to community learning. The former may drive out the latter.

Aligning College Work with Citizens' Work in Communities

So what has to happen to align the work of community colleges with the work of citizens? Do faculty have to leave the classroom and become community organizers? No. Alignment can be accomplished by educators

New Directions for Community Colleges • DOI: 10.1002/cc

doing what they normally do—just a bit differently. It is not a great stretch to incorporate what people hold dear with the expert names that professionals use. And it shouldn't be difficult to recognize all of the options for action that grow out of what citizens consider valuable. Exercising their faculty for judgment is something citizens, particularly students, should experience just as they should experience rational thought. And learning *with* not just *about* a community may be the most rewarding alignment of all because community colleges are all about learning.

The kind of alignment I am suggesting is already going on at some colleges that are using deliberative forums to reach both communities and students. (National Issues Forums are an example.) These forums create opportunities to name problems in people's terms, consider inclusive rather than bipolar frameworks, and exercise people's faculty for judgment. They are examples of better alignments.

Some of the forums have dealt with especially divisive, wicked problems, such as race relations. On these issues, the decisions have to do with more than facts; they have to do with what is right—for everybody. Such issues are seldom resolved through rational arguments. However, some communities have reduced tensions on volatile, wicked issues by developing a more deliberative climate. As you will recall, a deliberation framework recognizes different concerns that are at play and treats them all fairly. Deliberating also encourages people to recognize that differences over what is truly most important are often as much *within* individuals as they are *between* people. That recognition helps turn moral absolutes into practical political options.

When colleges have helped communities to create a more deliberative climate, the initiatives have often come from faculty members, not in response to an institutional requirement, but as a way of combining their academic careers with their public lives. We've been amazed at the variety of faculty who incorporate deliberative experiences into courses. Some are in fields where deliberation fits comfortably, such as speech communications and political science. There are also faculty in law, journalism, history, and science who are trying what they refer to as a *deliberative pedagogy*.

If deliberative experience is to receive academic credit, how is it to be evaluated? That's a difficult question. Yet there have been enough studies done already to show the positive effects of teaching with deliberation. The most exhaustive study was done by two professors at Wake Forest University, and although that is a 4-year institution, community college studies show similar effects. Katy Harriger and Jill McMillan created a Democracy Fellows program at Wake Forest to introduce students to citizen-centered, deliberative democracy. They used classroom instruction along with forums both on and off campus and reported the results in *Speaking of Politics* (Harriger & McMillan, 2007).

Programs like the one at Wake Forest open a door into politics for students who say that they don't know how to get meaningfully involved. They allow students to see how a democratic citizenry can move from hasty reactions to more shared and reflective judgment and how people can work together without being in full agreement. One Wake Forest graduate, reflecting on her experience, said that it had affected nearly everything she does. She learned how to become an effective political actor.

Significantly, the Wake Forest fellows were more, not less, likely to vote—even though they knew that elections are not the be-all and end-all of democracy. And unlike students who did not participate in the program, who thought of citizenship primarily as asserting individual rights, the fellows seemed more inclined to think of citizenship as collective problem solving.

What's at Stake?

Although this chapter has focused primarily on aligning the work of community colleges with the work of citizens and communities, I believe this alignment serves not only democracy but also the self-interest of the colleges. Today, nothing seems as important as giving students job skills at a reasonable price so that our economy will flourish in a competitive global market. Community colleges do that well, yet their standing as public institutions, as democracy's colleges, may be slipping—however unintentionally. In recent forums on the mission of colleges and universities, observers have been struck by how little was said about the public role of higher education.

A college degree is essential to most careers; still, focusing on individuals and their careers may give the impression that colleges and universities are moving away from their historic role of serving the public good. And if that happens, it will weaken these institutions' claim on public support. They become subject to the argument that if they give individuals only job skills, then those who benefit, not the public, should pay the costs. This is not a far-fetched possibility; tuition has been increasing while state funding—based on the public benefit of higher education—has declined. Reversing that trend will be difficult, but more evidence of a public role could help.

The most fundamental challenge that institutions of higher education face is to reestablish their public mandate! It is essential to their character and their legitimacy, just as it is essential to reclaiming a more robust understanding of democracy that returns citizens and their communities to the center.

References

Barber, B. (2003). *Strong democracy: Participatory politics for a new age* (2nd ed.). Berkeley: University of California Press.

Harriger, K., & McMillan, J. J. (2007). *Speaking of politics: Preparing college students for democratic citizenship through deliberative dialogue.* Dayton, OH: Kettering Foundation Press.

Mathews, D. (2014). *The ecology of democracy: Finding ways to have a stronger hand in shaping our future.* Dayton, OH: Kettering Foundation Press.

DAVID MATHEWS *is president of the Kettering Foundation. Themes explored in this chapter are drawn from a larger body of Kettering research on democracy and thus may appear in other writing by David Mathews.*

NEW DIRECTIONS FOR COMMUNITY COLLEGES • DOI: 10.1002/cc

4

This chapter describes the uncomfortable marriage between political science and civic education and calls for a reformulation of how we engage students in the wicked problems of democracy.

Political Science, Civic Engagement, and the Wicked Problems of Democracy

John J. Theis

Democracy in the United States is at a crossroads. National polls consistently show that not a single national political leader is viewed in a positive light on a consistent basis, and confidence in our political institutions is at record lows. In 2012 just 37% of respondents to a Gallup poll had "a great deal" or "quite a lot" of confidence in the institutions of the presidency or the Supreme Court, and only 13% thought similarly about Congress. This contrasts markedly with respondents' opinions when the question was first asked in 1975. At that time, the presidency stood at 52%, the Supreme Court at 49%, and Congress at 42%. In other words, in the aftermath of Watergate, U.S. political institutions were more highly regarded than they are some 40 years later.

Not only are we losing confidence in our political institutions, we are also losing confidence in each other. Indeed, Putnam (2000) and Ulsaner (2002) show that Americans have the lowest levels of trust in their fellow citizens and that these levels have been declining precipitously. Regardless of whom we elect and which policies get implemented, the public has become increasingly disillusioned, cynical, and apathetic, while problems continue to fester and grow. It seems that too many of those in charge are either incompetent, impotent, ignorant, in someone's pocket, or some combination of these. Partisan posturing, party gridlock, and an oft-noted decrease in civility among representatives from different parties reflect an adversarial approach to politics that is ill suited for the problems the United States faces in the 21st century.

New Directions for Community Colleges, no. 173, Spring 2016 © 2016 Wiley Periodicals, Inc.
Published online in Wiley Online Library (wileyonlinelibrary.com) • DOI: 10.1002/cc.20188

Civic Education in Colleges and Universities

At the same time that we are experiencing a crisis of confidence in our democratic institutions, the liberal arts in higher education have developed a crisis of legitimacy. People are questioning the value of broad-based liberal arts training in history, philosophy, and literature as our society moves increasingly toward a technocratic expert-driven culture. Community colleges have followed suit, emphasizing job training and workforce development over the broad-based learning demanded for educated citizens. We have forgotten John Adams's advice to his son: "You will ever remember that all the end of study is to make you a good man and a useful citizen" (Butterfield & Friedlaender, 1973, p. 117). When the Constitution's framers talked about education, they did not just mean vocational training or apprenticeships. "While this type of training was certainly important, they also wanted a citizenry trained in government, ethics (moral philosophy), history, rhetoric, science (natural philosophy), mathematics, logic, and classical languages, for these subjects made people informed and civil participants in a democratic society" (Fea, 2012, n.p.).

Early education reformers reflected this relationship between education and citizenship. Horace Mann, an early advocate for public education, explicitly contended that democracy requires educated citizens. John Dewey (1966), a leading reformer of public education at the turn of the century, said: "Democracy cannot flourish where the chief influences in selecting subject matter of instruction are utilitarian ends narrowly conceived for the masses, and, for the higher education of the few, the traditions of a specialized cultivated class" (p. 226). These authors seem more prescient than many would give them credit for, as civic engagement in our colleges and universities often feels very disconnected from—and secondary to—other, more prominent aims of 21st century higher education.

Civic education in most U.S. colleges has essentially taken one of three paths. It occurs in political science classes where one learns about institutions, parties, and voting—more on that soon. The second avenue for civic education at most U.S. colleges is in student life and in the amalgamation of student clubs and extracurricular activities that focus on citizenship and leadership. These are most often seen in college Democratic or Republican clubs, debate teams, get-out-the-vote drives, and student government. The final area of civic learning in higher education is volunteerism and service learning.

Very few of these civic activities in higher education see students as creators of their own civic lives; rather, they emphasize a passive or subordinate view of students in their communities. Indeed, these forms of political education on campus are about amassing facts and making expert arguments while lining up converts on your side rather than listening to different perspectives or interests and working toward a common solution. They are attempts to engage students in adversarial politics. Rather than helping students understand the full scope of potential roles for citizens, they reinforce the boxes that the broader culture puts citizens into and thus exacerbate the problems of democracy.

Political Science and Civic Education

Nowhere is this more apparent than in the discipline of political science. As Carcasson (2013) notes, "The bulk of the college experience focuses on the expert model... higher education is primarily tied to the notion of knowledge and data playing an important role in solving various problems" (p. 42). From a curricular perspective, civic education has been relegated to political science classes and unfortunately, as a discipline, it seems political science is ill equipped to handle it. The state of the political science field makes civic engagement an interloper on a broader scientific enterprise. Many modern theories of democracy actually eschew citizen involvement, arguing instead that passive apathetic citizens ensure stability of the political system and demonstrate citizen satisfaction with the status quo (Pateman, 1971). Almost no one makes the argument in mainstream political science journals that the lack of participation reflects a lack of democratic skills and that those skills must be learned (Boyte, 2001).

It hasn't always been this way. Early political theorists such as Mill and Rousseau saw participating in the process of democracy as helping to build a participatory character and participatory ethic, which would lead to increased legitimacy of the system. For them, a socialized norm of participation was essential to the functioning of democracy. Yet in an attempt to be *scientific*, today's political scientists have moved away from studying and grappling with a meaningful understanding of our role as citizens and the ways in which we act as agents in the political process. Instead they have reduced the citizen's role in our democratic political system to the easily quantifiable role of voter, a passive onlooker called upon once every few years to choose between competing decision makers. Although this is an exceedingly narrow definition of *citizen*, it fits a conception of democracy as a game for competing elites who derive their legitimacy from the adversarial politics of the voting booth.

This shift in the nature of political science resulted in part from a desire that it be taken seriously as a science, by a need to be objective and nonvalue based (this is reflected in the renaming of government departments into political science departments). The disciplinary shift is also reflected in the growth of empirical political science in which statistics and rational choice models have become the dominant paradigm.

With the 1951 publication of Kenneth Arrow's "Social Choice and Individual Values," conceptions of *Homo Economicus* began to make inroads into political science as a theory of choice. Arrow was rapidly followed by Downs' (1957) *An Economic Theory of Democracy* and Olson's (1965) *The Logic of Collective Action* to form the rational choice trifecta that every political science graduate student reads to enter the profession. Over the next 40 years, the number of rational choice-centered articles published in the *American Political Science Review*, the flagship journal of the American Political Science Association, grew from none to almost half of all articles (Green & Shapiro, 1994). Today, the tendency toward a rational choice-dominated field has not abated but it has stabilized. Of all the 2013 and 2014 articles appearing in the *American Political Science Review*, 49% either explicitly claimed a rational choice theoretical perspective or implicitly assumed it.

Why is this a problem for civic education? Within the rational choice framework, the issues of whether more people should participate in our democracy and how we encourage more participation are unasked questions; they are irrelevant because it is assumed that citizens must not see any expected utility from participating or else they would. Rational choice is an exceedingly conservative theology that prevents us from asking what *should be* or *might be* but permits studying only what *is*. For example, if people don't vote or attend neighborhood association meetings, the only permissible research question under this framework is why not. Researchers cannot ask whether people should do these things, what prevents them from doing them, or how might they be encouraged.

Politics is inherently a value-laden activity and trying to remove those values, I would argue, only drove them underground and out of sight. It isn't that there are no values in the dominant paradigm; it is only that they are not talked about. Rational choice implicitly assumes a normative framework and carries value judgments about political outcomes. As rational choice practitioners Riker and Ordeshook (1973) put it, "Society, not being human, cannot have preferences in any proper sense of 'have' nor indeed can it order the preferences it does not have" (p. 78). Thus with rational choice, political science entered a world where all preferences were merely the sum of individual preferences. Political science's dominant paradigm rejects the notion that individuals coming together may possess a different set of preferences as a group than the sum of their individual parts or that participating in a group may cause preferences to evolve or change. This assertion is made despite commonsense evidence to the contrary. Few people would argue that the actions of a family are simply the sum of individual preferences devoid of any collective interests. Although rational choice theory purports to be value free, the reality is that the perspective ends up positing a profoundly conservative set of values beneath the surface. Rational choice prevents—through its assumptions—any investigation into or questions about a common or collective good.

Furthermore, although rational choice models are inundating the political science literature, they fail to garner much support in the empirical world. When one looks at what the extensive rational choice literature has contributed to our understanding of politics, it is difficult not to be underwhelmed. As McKelvey and Rosenthal (1978) noted, it only rarely led to "rigorous empirical analysis of real world political behavior" (p. 405). Similarly, Fiorina (1976) said that the empirical achievements of rational choice theory are a little like "dwelling on the rushing accomplishments of Joe Namath" (p. 48). The literature on campaigns, elections, and voting behavior has in large part led to the empty and vacuous politics in which we find ourselves today, leaving so many with a deep dissatisfaction with our democracy. Rather than offering citizens the tools that they need to be better citizens and participate in our political system in a more powerful way, we have provided the tools that allow for the routine manipulation of citizens and reduced effectiveness in the political arena.

Thus political science has caused the marginalization of citizens in a political system where they should be front and center. If politics is just the sum of individual preferences, then experts only need to calculate solutions to problems that provide the largest net gain (maximization) of individual utilities. Also, advocates of policies need only to mobilize supporters on their side in order to increase the likelihood that their solution will be viewed as the one that maximizes utility. Politics becomes a numbers game with a technical solution. Yet this approach fails to account for the reality of today's problems. We inhabit a complex political world where people hold disparate values in varying intensities, and reconciling these entails many trade-offs and compromises. For political science to become relevant to the problems of democracy it needs a theory that understands the nature of contemporary democratic society and accounts for its complexity. Although not a theory, Rittel and Webber's (1973) conception of *wicked problems* can help to reconcile our approach to political science and civic education in colleges and universities with the problems of democracy.

Wicked Problems

In their foundational work, "Dilemmas in a General Theory of Planning," Rittel and Webber (1973) argued that "the professional's job was once seen as solving an assortment of problems that appeared to be definable, understandable, and consensual" (p. 156). But they go on to point out that "the professionalized cognitive and occupational styles that were refined in the first half of this century... are not readily adapted to contemporary conceptions of interacting open systems and to contemporary concerns with equity" (p. 156). They argue that today's problems are *wicked problems*. Wicked problems are those that are difficult or impossible to solve because they involve incomplete or contradictory knowledge, there are a large number of people and opinions involved, the large costs of solutions, and/or the interconnected nature of the problem with other problems (Rittel & Webber, 1973).

NEW DIRECTIONS FOR COMMUNITY COLLEGES • DOI: 10.1002/cc

Not only do wicked problems have no definitive meaning, but they have no definitive solutions according to standard technocratic measures of success. In other words, the solutions to wicked problems cannot be good or bad, true or false; they can only affect a problem and in turn give rise to additional spillover effects in other areas.

Nonetheless, Carcasson (2013) notes that "the tensions inherent in wicked problems can certainly be addressed in ways that are better or worse" (p. 38). He argues that "tackling wicked problems requires different forms of inquiry, communication, problem solving, and decision making than we often see on politics or public policy research" (p. 39). Both Carcasson (2013) and Roberts (2000) see three strategies for dealing with wicked problems.

First, the expert (authoritative) strategies seek to tame wicked problems by placing authority to make decisions in the hands of relatively small numbers of stakeholders, thus reducing the wickedness of the problem. The authorities define the problem and come up with a solution. Although this strategy has the advantage of reducing complexity and streamlining decision making (Roberts, 2000), its disadvantage lies in decisions having decreased legitimacy and less widespread acceptance.

The second strategy for dealing with wicked problems is the use of adversarial (competitive) strategies. Adversarial strategies, like a market, are zero sum—some interests will win whereas others will lose. These strategies have the advantage of being efficient, as competing solutions are evaluated through cost-benefit analysis and the one that maximizes utility is chosen. But this strategy can consume resources of the competing groups and the loser feels left out.

The third way to deal with wicked problems is through deliberative (collaborative) strategies that discard the zero sum mentality and instead adopt a win-win perspective. By involving stakeholders in deliberation and dialogue and reaching consensus, solutions to wicked problems can be implemented that maximize acceptance and legitimacy. Although more resources are required at the beginning as the problem comes to be defined and solutions are negotiated, implementation can proceed more smoothly with fewer resources involved in building support or strong-arming opponents.

Because wicked problems are value laden, they involve the basic reality of modern democracies: the need to involve a broad range of people and perspectives (Carcasson, 2013). Democracy, broadly viewed, is a mechanism for decision making among people who have a shared existence in space and time. Carcasson (2013) identifies deliberative engagement as the preferred mechanism for dealing with these problems of democracy: "Citizens come together and consider the relevant facts and values from multiple points of view, listen and react to one another in order to think critically about the various options before them, and ultimately attempt to work through the underlying tensions and tough choices inherent to wicked problems" (p. 41). Ultimately, the value-laden nature of wicked problems does not make their solution amenable to a simple aggregation of preferences in the manner rational choice literature suggests. In the end, a more nuanced and complex vision of decision making in a democracy is needed to help deal with these problems.

Civic Engagement

A focus on wicked problems also moves our efforts away from civic *education* and toward civic *engagement*. This is a popular idea; in recent years civic engagement has become a buzzword in higher education. Schools have been renaming their service learning programs civic engagement programs; Campus Compact now claims to be doing civic engagement, and scholars are writing about service learning as a kind of civic engagement. Service learning is out and civic engagement is in. Yet as so often happens, much of the emphasis on civic engagement is simply old wine being poured into new bottles. As Saltmarsh (2005) astutely notes, much civic education focuses on service and volunteerism. For service learning to be engagement, it must wed academic rigor with real civic experiences; it must advance students' knowledge of course materials by "connecting subject interests with civic participation, inculcating the value of civic participation, and teaching skills for productive civic participation" (McCartney, 2013, p. 15). Clearly, the fact that people feel the need to clarify service learning with the words "proper" or "done right" indicates the degree to which we must move beyond service learning to provide students with positive civic experiences that do not reduce to volunteerism. Service stresses a person's contribution in a nonpolitical manner—it emphasizes helping the less fortunate out of a sense of noblesse oblige—whereas civic engagement stresses student agency and power in caring for the health of the community.

The challenge for any institution of higher learning is to get beyond contemporary forms of political education—whether that be a lecture-based government class, party-affiliated student clubs, or volunteerism—and learn to tie rich civic experiences to concepts and skills from across the curriculum. As Ronan (2011) points out, civic engagement must move the whole person along a continuum from civics, voting, and patriotism toward deliberation, concord, and public action. Deliberation, concord, and public action are crucial to civic engagement because they provide students with the skills to tackle the problems of democracy. As Ronan notes, these three concepts are deeper and more transformative and thus get closer to the ideas that Mill and Rousseau thought participation in the system would bring. Institutions of higher education can and should provide students with the experience-based skills that are necessary for deliberation, concord, and public action and essential for solving the wicked problems of democracy. Ultimately, for real civic engagement to occur, our century-old model of lecture-driven education, our preoccupation with rational choice frameworks in political science, and a few extracurricular opportunities for political involvement and volunteering will have to give way to a more holistic notion of civic education that seamlessly incorporates democratic practices across the campus, from the classrooms, to the dorms, and the community beyond.

References

Arrow, K. J. (1951). *Social choice and individual values*. New Haven, CT: Yale University Press.

Boyte, H. C. (2001, August–September). *A tale of two playgrounds: Young people and politics*. Paper presented at the annual meeting of the American Political Science Association, San Francisco, CA.

Butterfield, L. H., & Friedlaender, M., (Eds.). (1973). John Adams to John Quincy Adams, 18 May 1781. *The Adams papers, Adams family correspondence, vol. 4, October 1780–September 1782* (pp. 117–118). Cambridge, MA: Harvard University Press.

Carcasson, M. (2013). Rethinking civic engagement on campus: The overarching potential of deliberative practice. Higher Education Exchange, 37–48.

Dewey, J. (1966). *Democracy and education: An introduction to the philosophy of education*. New York: Free Press.

Downs, A. (1957). *An economic theory of democracy*. New York: Harper & Row.

Fea, J. (2012, Mar. 13). Education for a democracy. *Patheos*. Retrieved from http://www.patheos.com/Resources/Additional-Resources/Education-for-a-Democracy-John-Fea-03-14-2012.html.

Fiorina, M. P. (1976). The voting decision: Instrumental and expressive aspects. *Journal of Politics, 38*(2), 390–413.

Green, D. P., & Shapiro, I. (1994). *Pathologies of rational choice theory: A critique of applications in political science*. New Haven, CT: Yale University Press.

McCartney, A. R. M. (2013). Teaching civic engagement: Debates, definitions, benefits, and challenges. In A. R. M. McCartney, E. A. Bennion, & D. Simpson (Eds.), *Teaching civic engagement: From student to active citizen* (pp. 9–20). Washington, DC. American Political Science Association.

McKelvey, R. D., & Rosenthal, H. (1978). Coalition formation, policy distance, and the theory of games without side payments: An application to the French apparentement system. In P. C. Ordeshook (Ed.), *Game theory and political science*. New York: New York University Press.

Olson, M. (1965). *The logic of collective action*. Cambridge, MA: Harvard University Press.

Pateman, C. (1976). *Participation and democratic theory*. Cambridge, UK: Cambridge University Press.

Putnam, R. D. (2000). *Bowling alone: The collapse and revival of American community*. New York: Simon and Schuster.

Riker, W., & Ordeshook, P. C. (1973). *Introduction to positive political theory*. Englewood Cliffs, NJ: Prentice Hall.

Rittel, H. W. J., & Webber, M. M. (1973). Dilemmas in a general theory of planning. *Policy Sciences, 4*(2), 155–169.

Roberts, N. (2000). Wicked problems and network approaches to resolution. *International Public Management Review, 1*(1), 1–19.

Ronan, B. (2011). *The civic spectrum: How students become engaged citizens*. Dayton, OH: Kettering Foundation.

Saltmarsh, J. (2005). The civic promise of service learning. *Liberal Education, 91*(2), 50–55.

Ulsaner, E. M. (2002). *The moral foundations of trust*. New York: Cambridge University Press.

JOHN J. THEIS is professor of political science at Lone Star College-Kingwood, Texas.

This chapter explores the leadership qualities participants identified as pivotal to the development of civic engagement at a large, suburban community college.

Civic Engagement and Cosmopolitan Leadership

Clifford P. Harbour

In spring 2011, senior leaders at Forest View Community College (FVCC, a pseudonym) decided to explore membership in The Democracy Commitment (TDC), a new national initiative designed to help U.S. community colleges educate their students for democracy. Upon the recommendation of a small exploratory committee, FVCC's president appointed a planning committee to assess the fit between TDC and FVCC. Over the next 3½ years, FVCC's faculty, staff, and students created a unique civic engagement program that became integrated into the campus culture, although not without challenges and controversy. This chapter describes an important dimension of this development—the shared leadership qualities that participants viewed as pivotal to the program's early success.

This chapter derives from an interpretative, structure-focused case study conducted at FVCC in September 2014. As part of this investigation, I interviewed formal and informal leaders; observed students, faculty, and staff; and analyzed pertinent documents. After a brief discussion of the relevant literature and the study's research methods, this chapter describes the leadership qualities associated with the success of FVCC's TDC program. These leadership qualities fall into three themes and are captured most aptly by a concept I call *cosmopolitan leadership*. Cosmopolitan leadership includes both descriptive and normative components and is informed by Appiah's (2007) notion of *cosmopolitanism*. For Appiah, cosmopolitans acknowledge the reality that "different people and different societies will embody different values" (p. 144), but they also place faith in the notion that there are universal truths that transcend communities and acknowledge that these truths must be discovered, learned, and used to develop

New Directions for Community Colleges, no. 173, Spring 2016 © 2016 Wiley Periodicals, Inc.
Published online in Wiley Online Library (wileyonlinelibrary.com) • DOI: 10.1002/cc.20189

a better society. In short, cosmopolitans value difference but cherish our common humanity.

Civic Engagement in the Literature

The literature on the evolution of civic engagement at U.S. colleges and universities is extensive. Some of these works have highlighted the demise of civic learning in the nation and its higher education institutions (e.g., Kanter & Schneider, 2013). Others have described the constellation of national civic engagement programs and movements that have been advanced to counter this demise (e.g., Hartley, 2011; Thomas & Levine, 2011). And blue ribbon panels such as the National Task Force on Civic Learning and Democratic Engagement (2012) have proposed institutional frameworks for a renewed commitment to civic engagement on college campuses.

A review of the literature confirms that in U.S. higher education, traditional commitments to civic learning and democratic engagement have been weakened by the prioritization of professional, commercial, and career curricula (Bond & Paterson, 2005). This change in priorities has been rationalized by the neoliberal belief that the primary purpose of higher education should be to promote individual financial success and state economic development. Preparing students for an active role in their democracy is of secondary importance. Notwithstanding this context, many community colleges are renewing or expanding their commitment to civic engagement, as many of the chapters in this volume attest.

Research Methods

In June 2014, I contacted TDC national leaders and expressed an interest in studying the leadership associated with a TDC college that was viewed as successful by peer institutions. TDC leaders identified five community colleges for possible study. Each of the five had a national reputation for developing high-quality civic engagement programs. After conducting an online investigation of all five, I selected FVCC because of its national prominence, its history of civic engagement programming, and an invitation from the president to conduct the study at their campus. To investigate the leadership qualities associated with a successful community college civic engagement program, I used an interpretive, structure-focused qualitative case study method. This method is well suited for investigations examining the perceptions of individuals working in complex social units (Merriam, 2009; Patton, 2014). I began data collection in July 2014 by gathering texts describing FVCC and its TDC program. I then consulted two senior leaders at FVCC. These activities led to the identification of a nominated sample of formal and informal leaders familiar with the development of FVCC's TDC program. In September 2014, I spent 4 days touring the FVCC campus and service area, conducting interviews, and collecting additional documents.

Ten full-time FVCC employees agreed to be privately interviewed and audio recorded. These included the president, the vice presidents (VPs) of instruction and student development, the two cochairs of FVCC's TDC committee, the TDC faculty coordinator, the campus environment and sustainability manager, an admissions officer, a political science professor, and the dean of students. Five of the 10 participants were African American, four were White, and one participant declined to self-identify. Six of the 10 participants were female. Participant work experience at FVCC ranged from 3 to 26 years. Following a semistructured interview format, each participant was asked to describe his or her career in community college education, experience at FVCC, and involvement in the establishment of the TDC program. Participants were then asked to reflect on the leadership qualities they observed and associated with the establishment and development of the program.

The Evolution of Civic Engagement at FVCC

FVCC is a comprehensive community college that enrolls approximately 35,000 credit and noncredit students (unduplicated headcount). It employs 200 full-time and 600 part-time faculty and offers over 100 programs leading to a certificate or an associate degree. The campus is located 25 miles from the downtown business district of a very large city in the continental United States. The city has a very diverse population, a broad array of industries, and a world-class higher education community.

In 2011 and 2012, members of the TDC planning committee met extensively with constituencies on and off campus. At open meetings across campus, faculty, staff, and students listened to their peers and discussed the need for a TDC program. One member of the TDC planning committee, the VP for student development (we'll call her Kimura; all other names have been changed as well) met with more than 20 local municipal leaders to explain what TDC was and how FVCC leaders were considering creation of an affiliate at their college.

Initially, some faculty suspected the initiative was intended to promote a liberal or progressive political agenda. But after campus meetings and continued dialogue, this suspicion declined. Most faculty and staff agreed that a more focused and deliberate commitment to civic engagement was appropriate and could provide students with valuable learning experiences. Eventually, the president and other senior leaders decided that FVCC was "all in" on TDC and created a formal TDC committee, which was cochaired by the assistant deans of student life and liberal arts. These two cochairs convened a group of 15 staff, faculty, and students, cofacilitating monthly meetings. Over the next 2 years, the TDC committee endorsed service learning projects and sponsored or cosponsored activities such as the Oxfam America Hunger Banquet, the One Book One Campus Program, and an on-campus citizenship naturalization ceremony.

Participants agreed that FVCC had a robust array of civic engagement activities prior to the formation of the TDC committee. Service learning activities, embedded in the curriculum, had been offered since 2001. An FVCC Global Education Initiative and an International Education Initiative also supported activities encouraging civic engagement. As one participant explained, the TDC initiative was adopted not because it would take the college in a new direction, but because it aligned with an existing commitment to promote civic engagement and, therefore, was "a good thing for our campus and our students." Still, development of a TDC program represented a new frontier in civic engagement for FVCC.

Leading for Civic Engagement

When I analyzed the transcript data, three themes emerged: active, adaptive, and resilient leadership; learning for leadership; and engagement for the greater good.

Active, Adaptive, and Resilient Leadership. Echoing the literature on institutionalizing civic engagement at community colleges (Kisker & Ronan, 2012), Carmen, the VP for instruction, explained some of the lessons learned in developing FVCC's TDC program:

> The first thing you have to have is commitment from the president because it really needs to be initiated from the top in order to have the campus community take part and engage. I think [faculty and staff] have to know that there is a commitment from the president and the executive leaders to understand that this is an important topic, a topic that we care about, support and want to promote. ... The second thing you have to do is get everyone involved, that's another condition. It can't just be faculty; it can't just be staff. ... It has to be everyone. So you have to have opportunities where people are educated about it and understand, and then you have to teach them how they actually take part and be a part of it. Another condition is that you have to have resources to support it—whether its sending faculty or staff off to conferences, hosting speakers on campus, hosting events, things like marketing (fliers, videos). ... And another condition would be meeting space, and then making space available on campus so that these things can happen. ... Those are the things that I would say are really important in making it successful. And then last but not least, making sure that you have the right people as the leaders of the team.

Carmen and other participants acknowledged that TDC committee members possessed the traditional organizational, interpersonal, and communication skills needed to create a new program. But they agreed that these were not sufficient to develop and sustain a robust civic engagement program. Instead, they cited the necessary qualities of active, adaptive, and resilient leadership.

For example, Bernice, the sustainability manager, explained that TDC committee members made a "proactive effort" to support campus programs and activities that might help develop a sense of civic awareness and community. Similarly, Kimura, the VP for student development, explained that her role in developing the TDC program was "to be a catalyst. So my job as senior administrator was to help the faculty and the employees make things happen, that was my job. And what's my other job? It's to remove any foreseeable barriers." Other participants added that their work on the TDC committee was focused on moving the program forward. Kathleen, the TDC coordinator, was especially active in promoting the program. Besides working as a faculty member in the English department, in 2014 Kathleen hosted or facilitated seven activities on campus, was a keynote speaker at a civic engagement event held at a nearby university, and presented at the national TDC conference.

Participants also described a leadership approach that emphasized the importance of flexibility and adaptation. They observed that as a new initiative at FVCC, the TDC program needed to find its place at a very busy college. TDC committee members actively engaged with faculty, staff, and student leaders to explain TDC events and to ensure that they fit into a campus schedule that had to accommodate activities sponsored by more than 30 student clubs. Kathleen's flexibility as a leader was noted by several of her colleagues. As Bernice explained, "She's very adaptive. She's also intentional, and extremely passionate, and you can see it, she really believes in the TDC program and the values within. ... [She leads] in a democratic way. And there are others on the team who are like that."

Other participants attributed the success of the TDC program to formal and informal leaders who, perhaps above all else, were resilient. Elizabeth, the TDC committee cochair, acknowledged that the group encountered challenges in crafting the TDC program's mission statement, in developing consensus on the direction and speed of the program, and in interacting with the occasional faculty member who suspected a more political and less transparent agenda. But the TDC committee rebounded whenever progress was temporarily stalled. As Elizabeth explained, "We were persistent on getting that thing done. We were definitely persistent." *Active, adaptive, and resilient leadership* was the first and most transparent theme that emerged in the study.

Learning for Leadership. A second theme that emerged in data analysis was *learning for leadership*. The overall purpose of FVCC's TDC program evolved through organized discussions among students, faculty, and staff. And, as mentioned, members of the FVCC community began to view the civic engagement program as an opportunity to strengthen their existing efforts in service learning, campus sustainability, global education, and a campus commitment to value and celebrate diversity. The intention was not so much to create but to integrate high-quality learning experiences under the umbrella of a more focused civic engagement agenda. A critical component of this focus was the belief that students needed to understand the U.S. political system, the economic system, and the larger society. With this understanding, they could then learn the skills needed to advocate for themselves in these different contexts. In this regard, the student experience that participants desired was holistic and deliberately focused on developing students' capacity to become leaders and advocates, not just for their own needs and interests but for others in their community. Participants in this study, therefore, wanted a civic engagement program that had an impact on the entire FVCC community—not just the students. They intentionally embedded these priorities in campus civic engagement activities.

This last point was reflected in comments made by Sullivan, the TDC committee cochair. He explained, "I think that the education part is not only about educating people that we think aren't involved [students], but educating those people who think they are involved [faculty and staff]. And so educating all of us rather than just [students]." He went on to note that there are those who think they know everything, but he asked rhetorically, "Are they well rounded or are they focused just on one thing?" Interviews with other participants confirmed that they viewed a good civic engagement program as one that did more than educate students about the political process or provide a service to the community. A good civic engagement program needed to offer all members of the FVCC community—and especially students—experiences that would help them learn to lead in a variety of community settings and organizations.

Engagement for the Greater Good.   The third theme that emerged was *engagement for the greater good*. Participants acknowledged that it was important to help everyone learn how to play a constructive role in their political democracy and create a happy and productive life for themselves. As Kathleen explained, "Civic engagement is more than going to vote. Civic engagement must also provide students with access to a quality of life, however you define that quality of life."

Kathleen continued by noting that life in a democracy involves interacting with different people leading very different lives. What makes some communities happy, enriching places is the ability of community members to directly acknowledge problems and deal with them in a respectful and constructive manner. She noted that in some cases "democracy is uncomfortable," but the best communities address their problems and work through them for the greater good.

Participants recognized that helping students understand the importance of working for the greater good could not be relegated to classroom instruction. The lessons we learn about *why* the greater good is important and *how* we can work to realize this ideal are often grounded in life experiences—not textbooks. Samantha, FVCC's president and a 64-year-old African-American woman, strongly supported the college's TDC program and saw it as an essential component of what community college education must be in the 21st century. But for her, the importance of civic engagement was affirmed by what she had learned in life. She told me:

> I'll be honest with you, my understanding of why civic engagement is important comes not only from my role as an educator now, but also from my experiences as a person growing up in the United States. And because of my own background and my parents' and grandparents' backgrounds, I know you need to have a voice in the decisions about how your country is shaped and developed. ... Everybody needs to be engaged in the civic process, not just for themselves but, for others. ... I think people who understand what [civic engagement] is about, are doing it for the greater good. You know, this work is really about creating a society that is good for everybody. So the faculty and staff who are involved in this see this as something bigger than just the class that they teach or the program that they run. They see this as "we can actually have some influence and some part in the world of creating a better society ... we are doing it for the greater good." So this project, this commitment, is about the students, it's about helping the students, it's about the greater good of the community. ... It's about being able to be who you want to be, to be able to express yourself, to be able to be free, to have equal opportunity ... I don't even want to call it a project anymore, you know, it's becoming embedded in our college culture. ... I hope our students will leave here with the understanding that they too can make a difference, that they have been given an opportunity to make a difference.

As Samantha spoke these words, her passion for a greater good reinforced the intellectual argument she was making. She looked back on her life and career as one filled with great challenges but also great rewards. In her view, the TDC program was becoming a part of the way teaching and learning was lived at FVCC. And the activities sponsored and supported by the TDC program provided students—and also faculty and staff—with the opportunity to learn how to live better lives in their community.

Cosmopolitan Leadership

After I completed my last interview at FVCC, I left directly for the airport. As I waited for my evening flight home, I noticed a long line of large jets, all international carriers, parked at the concourse gates. Passengers were boarding flights to Paris, London, Brussels, Mexico City, Tokyo. Many appeared to be seasoned travelers, with the fashionable dress and travel accessories any of us might associate with sophisticated cosmopolitans.

As I sat in the terminal, the image of my last day at FVCC returned to me. That morning, I had prepared for my interviews in the cafeteria alongside a diverse group of students, faculty, and staff hunkered over their coffee and tea and focused on their books and laptops. Now I was in a major international airport, tired but happy to be heading home. I realized that the cosmopolitans I saw in the concourse were, in some respects, quite similar to the people I observed in the FVCC cafeteria. They were citizens of the world and had come to FVCC from many different nations and communities.

Several weeks later, in a follow-up interview with the president, Samantha, I shared my experiences of my last day on campus and my sense that FVCC students, faculty, and staff were quite cosmopolitan in their own right. Not the cosmopolitanism of well-to-do international travelers, but the cosmopolitanism of a community that understands—as Appiah (2007) states, that "human beings are different and that we can learn from each other's differences" (p. 4). "Yes" Samantha agreed, "the campus does have a cosmopolitan atmosphere."

Reading the transcripts again, I began to see that cosmopolitan leadership, for these participants, did not discount the importance of organizational skills, interpersonal skills, or communication skills. But these leaders saw the college's TDC program as something that guided teaching and learning in ways that aligned with core values that had long been at the heart of the institution. This, perhaps, illuminates a power of The Democracy Commitment not only as a programmatic mechanism to help community colleges transform existing or develop new civic engagement programming, but also as a force that can nourish and expand commitments to democracy that are already in place at U.S. community colleges.

Conclusion

Cosmopolitan leadership at FVCC defied an easy explanation. Participants declined to identify a single leader as the sustaining force of the program. The leadership qualities they associated with the TDC program were shared and distributed across many members. But what pervaded participant interviews was the recognition that FVCC was something special, an effective, very diverse higher education institution that included many different people with many different values. Along with this descriptive component, however, was the normative belief that FVCC's diversity was a strength that could help students, faculty, and staff learn to become participants in a democracy in ways that improved upon and expanded beyond mere political participation. Teaching and learning at FVCC certainly included a heavy commitment to success in the workplace and a recognition that continued economic development was important. But—spurred on by the TDC program—the FVCC campus culture now embraced experiences and opportunities for all to learn how they might become more engaged in the political, economic, and social dimensions of the community. And beyond this was the hope that everyone might also learn how to play a role in achieving the greater good.

References

Appiah, K. A. (2007). *Cosmopolitanism: Ethics in a world of strangers*. New York: W. W. Norton.

Bond, R., & Paterson, L. (2005). Coming down from the ivory tower? Academics' civic and economic engagement with the community. *Oxford Review of Education, 31*(3), 331–351.

Hartley, M. (2011). Idealism and compromise and the civic engagement movement. In J. Saltmarsh & M. Hartley (Eds.), *"To serve a larger purpose": Engagement for democracy and the transformation of higher education* (pp. 27–48). Philadelphia, PA: Temple University Press.

Kanter, M., & Schneider, C. G. (2013). Civic learning and engagement. *Change, 45*(1), 6–14.

Kisker, C. B., & Ronan, B. (2012). *Civic engagement in community colleges. Mission, institutionalization, and future prospects*. Dayton, OH: Kettering Foundation.

Merriam, S. B. (2009). *Qualitative research: A guide to design and implementation*. San Francisco: Jossey-Bass.

National Task Force on Civic Learning and Democratic Engagement. (2012). *A crucible moment: College learning and democracy's future*. Washington, DC: Association of American Colleges and Universities.

Patton, M. Q. (2014). *Qualitative research & evaluation methods: Integrating theory and practice* (4th ed.). Thousand Oaks, CA: Sage.Thomas, N., & Levine, P. (2011). Deliberative democracy and higher education. In J. Saltmarsh & M. Hartley (Eds.), *"To serve a larger purpose": Engagement for democracy and the transformation of higher education* (pp. 154–176). Philadelphia, PA: Temple University Press.

CLIFFORD P. HARBOUR *is professor of adult and postsecondary education at the University of Wyoming.*

NEW DIRECTIONS FOR COMMUNITY COLLEGES • DOI: 10.1002/cc

6

This chapter describes the process and challenges of implementing a civic engagement graduation requirement at Kingsborough Community College.

Implementing the Civic Engagement Graduation Requirement at Kingsborough Community College

Lavita McMath Turner

Across the country, community colleges are demonstrating a strong commitment to the civic learning and democratic engagement of their students. However, few colleges have institutionalized their commitment across all disciplines and for the benefit of all students. Over the past few years, Kingsborough Community College (KCC) has sought to do just that. In fall 2008, former KCC President Regina Peruggi challenged members of her administration to think about how every student could be "touched by civic engagement" and established Kingsborough's Civic Engagement Advisory Committee to explore how the college might provide opportunities for students to actively explore societal issues through diverse, valuable, and innovative educational experiences. The committee broadly represented the college community and included faculty as well as administrators from academic affairs, student affairs, continuing education, and government relations. With the assistance of a consultant, the committee reviewed various definitions of civic engagement and examined various liberal education as well as civic and experiential learning models. We conducted a civic engagement survey and found that many forms of civic learning were already taking place all over the campus. However, we learned that the majority of these activities focused on particular student populations such as honors, student government, or full-time day students.

As a result of this examination, the committee decided that the only way to ensure that every student—irrespective of academic performance, enrollment status, or level of campus involvement—was touched by civic engagement was to establish a civic engagement graduation requirement.

New Directions for Community Colleges, no. 173, Spring 2016 © 2016 Wiley Periodicals, Inc.
Published online in Wiley Online Library (wileyonlinelibrary.com) • DOI: 10.1002/cc.20190

The committee also approved a definition of civic engagement that would guide this initiative:

> Kingsborough accepts as a fundamental principle that education requires social awareness, an acceptance of social responsibility and active participation in meeting the challenges of a modern society. Through civic engagement, we recognize our mutual responsibility to care for each other in the college, in our communities, and on our planet. This responsibility may be accomplished through political activity, community service, engagement in leadership roles, advocacy or becoming informed on issues which relate to social change.

KCC's civic engagement graduation requirement—which began in fall 2013 for entering students and those changing majors—mandates that students complete two civic engagement (CE) experiences before graduating. These two experiences can be satisfied by *certified CE courses* (courses where the nature or content includes civic engagement as an essential learning outcome); *component CE courses* (courses in which some of the content or activities are devoted to civic engagement and where there are opportunities to link academic concepts to a commitment to the community; and/or *cocurricular activities*, such as volunteering or participating in student government or other leadership development activities.

As director of government relations at KCC, I took a leadership role in the implementation of KCC's civic education graduation requirement, which relies heavily on full-time faculty and staff to teach certified component CE courses and to lead cocurricular activities. I had expected that— given the results of our campus civic engagement survey—the full-timers would be ready and able to participate in the new requirement. However, a number of unexpected internal challenges challenged the implementation of the requirement. This chapter details the major issues that surfaced, providing examples along the way. It also describes the processes we established to address these issues, focusing on what worked (and what didn't). The chapter concludes with an analysis of lessons learned at Kingsborough and our next steps for implementing and institutionalizing the civic engagement graduation requirement.

Questions and Concerns About the New Graduation Requirement

As KCC's graduation requirement was implemented in fall 2013, three key questions or concerns emerged among faculty and staff. First, it became clear that some full-time faculty, staff, and administrators did not readily see the intrinsic nature of civic engagement at community colleges, and similarly, the value of civic learning for all our students. Second, some full-time faculty lacked clarity on what civic engagement *is* and how it can be integrated into the various disciplines. In particular, many were highly

NEW DIRECTIONS FOR COMMUNITY COLLEGES • DOI: 10.1002/cc

concerned that the civic engagement requirement would merely be an "add-on" instead of a pedagogical tool. Finally, some full-time faculty had difficulty recognizing civic outcomes as "traditional" learning outcomes.

Why Do We Need a Campuswide Focus on Civic Engagement? This question—much to my surprise—dominated much of the discourse at KCC during the implementation process and still continues to do so. Civic engagement advisers had difficulty explaining the concept, and moreover, once the requirement was in place, faculty began to express concerns about how to do it, which led to back to the question of why civic engagement was necessary for all students. Many faculty—especially those who were already interested in civic engagement work—wondered why they couldn't just work with those students who wanted to be civically engaged. And indeed, despite KCC's active service learning program, many cocurricular activities, and numerous faculty-initiated civic projects across the campus, all of the students in these programs had self-selected into them and were often high-achieving students such as those in our honors program. There was an underlying feeling among faculty that many of our students wouldn't be interested in this type of learning and that the college should focus just on traditional subject matter and skills needed for transfer or obtaining a job. Embedded in this assumption is the notion that perhaps developmental-level students don't need the added pressure of learning about concepts of advocacy, political knowledge, and social responsibility if they can't yet read, write, and compute at a college level.

In order to address this issue, as well as others detailed later in this chapter, I collaborated with faculty in the Civic Engagement Faculty Interest Group and the Bridging Cultures Project, as well as the Teagle Foundation. These faculty became an unofficial cadre of civic engagement faculty ambassadors. They assisted by facilitating conversations both formally and informally with their colleagues. I also conducted informational sessions with college advisers and registrar staff and presented at departmental and chairs meetings. In particular, I spent a lot of time talking about how engaging *all* students in civic learning is expressly linked to the long-standing civic and democratic mission of community colleges. Although I cannot report that these conversations have persuaded all of KCC's faculty and staff that civic skills are necessary for all of our students, I believe that many more of my colleagues now understand why we need a campuswide focus on civic engagement.

What Is Civic Engagement and How Can It Be Integrated into the Classroom? Another issue that arose during the implementation of KCC's civic engagement graduation requirement was confusion about the definition of civic engagement and what constitutes a civic experience. For example, is service learning the same as civic engagement? If students aren't given an off-campus assignment or required volunteer activity, is it really civic engagement? How can civic engagement be integrated into the syllabus without taking away from the purity of the subject matter?

New Directions for Community Colleges • DOI: 10.1002/cc

Civic engagement and our particular definition of it has been a cause of concern among some faculty. Many have had a hard time understanding the intent of KCC's definition, which is to allow for flexibility in how civic engagement is actually carried out by faculty and staff and to accommodate learning in and out of the classroom and within the complex lives of our students.

Instead, the definition is viewed by many as too liberal or overreaching or as something that could be used to justify anything loosely resembling civic engagement. Furthermore, in various meetings, faculty expressed concern that the definition might lead to the imposition of values on students, especially those of a political nature.

In order to address these concerns, the committee—with the support of staff in the academic affairs department—created an informational sheet about the graduation requirement and are working to improve the collegewide civic engagement website that will include professional development materials. However, it is clear that these actions will not fully alleviate concerns about what civic engagement means or how the expression of political ideas can and should be expressed on campus. These are issues that we will be working to address in the coming years.

Are Civic Learning Objectives Legitimate, and Are They Assessed the Same as "Traditional" Learning Objectives? Conversations with faculty—even those tasked with approving certified CE courses— demonstrated confusion about how to incorporate civic engagement pedagogy into their teaching in ways that recognize civic outcomes as legitimate. For example, numerous faculty who teach a course that has been designated as certified CE based on its content still did not understand how the civic domains that the course met—such as social responsibility, political knowledge, or advocacy—could be integrated into their existing learning outcomes and graded or assessed similarly. Some believed that the civic engagement outcomes should be held to a separate or different grading standard that could explicitly demonstrate an increase in civic engagement.

Faculty who teach service learning courses are often more clear in their assessment of civic learning outcomes because this specific pedagogy relies heavily on an actual participation in an activity accompanied by a reflection paper. Faculty who use a traditional teaching style with an emphasis on the textbook and accompanying instructor materials appear to be the most uncomfortable with a civic engagement focus. This concern has even led some within the college community to rethink the concept of certifying particular courses and instead certifying specific faculty.

Although the reason for certifying all introductory sociology courses as CE courses made sense based upon departmental course descriptions and topics of the suggested textbooks (which included culture and social structure, inequalities of race and ethnicity, political and economic power, and social change), there is understandably some discomfort with assuming that all instructors of introductory sociology will teach it in a way that

encourages students to think critically about current issues of social strat-
ification, power, deviance, and race and gender, or in ways that may lead
to advocacy, increased political knowledge, or acts of social responsibility.
This type of teaching requires a certain level of comfort that may take time
for faculty to develop. However, for some faculty a greater focus on civic
engagement may be freeing. As one professor stated, this project allowed
her to teach the way she always wanted, which was from a social justice
perspective.

To address this issue, we have focused our attention on strengthening
our Civic Engagement Faculty Interest Group, which is led by one of our
long-time civic engagement faculty ambassadors. I have also been working with one department to gather engagement resources that can be made
available on their website and that can serve as a model for other departments. This effort is being done in conjunction with a redesign of the Center
for Civic Engagement website, which will store all relevant resources and
materials, and coincides with KCC's Center for Civic Engagement moving
to its permanent location and a campaign to raise awareness of all of the
civic activities occurring on campus.

Lessons Learned and Next Steps

Two years after the implementation of Kingsborough Community College's
civic engagement graduation requirement, I have had some time to reflect
on the process and identify some approaches or tactics that worked well, as
well as some that—had we used them—would have made our process run
more smoothly. The first lesson learned is by far the hardest, because its
implications are far reaching: *The need to engage all students in civic learning should be expressly linked to the long-standing civic mission of community
colleges in the beginning of the process through a collegewide dialogue.* This is
particularly important given what I perceive to be an emergence of philosophical differences among faculty regarding the importance of civic learning and citizenship development for community college students. I'm not
sure how many more faculty KCC could have won over if we had more explicitly linked these two ideas at the onset of our implementation process,
but at least it would have provided an historical context for pursuing this
agenda and diminished the appearance of it being solely an administrative
initiative or administrative interference in academic issues.

Without such a dialogue, the college community as a whole failed to
realize several key points necessary for embracing this initiative:

1. Community college students are uniquely qualified to think critically
   about issues that affect their communities and our society using different subject matter and disciplines.
2. Civic engagement provides us with an opportunity to offer a real-
   world context for liberal arts education. This may be especially

important, as mainstream media regularly report that students from all backgrounds—especially those from disadvantaged and marginalized communities—question the relevance of college amid ever-increasing costs.

3. A commitment to civic and global learning is imperative for a college such as KCC, which is located in the cultural capital of the world and has a student population representing 142 different countries and over 70 different languages.

A second lesson learned is that faculty who might be predisposed for work of a civic or social justice nature should be brought in as ambassadors early in the process. This is something that KCC did somewhat well. Over the past few years, we identified numerous KCC faculty who are not only civically engaged themselves, but who are also comfortable engaging their students in activities and discussions that develop civic capacities. The recruitment of these faculty as civic engagement ambassadors contributed greatly to our ongoing development and refinement of policies and procedures related to the graduation requirement. These faculty have also shared teaching strategies internally and externally through conferences, scholarly publications, and participation in national civic engagement research projects.

A final lesson learned is that a comprehensive public relations campaign focused on the ways in which civic engagement can be institutionalized across the campus and its curricula is necessary in order to dispel confusion about what civic engagement is and how faculty can incorporate it. If KCC had implemented such a public relations campaign at the start of the implementation process, we could have reduced some of the confusion we see today, and everyone in our community—staff, students, full- and part-time faculty—could have become more knowledgeable about civic engagement and why there is a need to align our programs and activities with our civic mission as a community college. Although KCC did not make such a push at the onset of implementation, we have begun to catch up through ongoing training of faculty and staff. These trainings occur in departmental and chairs meetings, as well as in faculty interest groups, and they have been critical to ensuring the success of our agenda.

Since the implementation of the civic engagement graduation requirement, many more faculty have expressed interest in creating opportunities for students both inside and outside the classroom. I believe this is due in part to the increased national attention to civic learning and the funding opportunities available in this area. Additionally, the recent unfortunate incidents in this country involving the police or people acting in authority and men of color have led to greater interest across the campus community in examining issues of equity, diversity, and social justice. Perhaps as a result of this national conversation, as well as the efforts of KCC's civic engagement advisory committee and many others, more faculty and staff

NEW DIRECTIONS FOR COMMUNITY COLLEGES • DOI: 10.1002/cc

are seeking information about how to incorporate civic engagement into their classes and activities with students. Many have indicated that they already do this, but didn't know it. Some are asking for help in adjusting their syllabus and teaching style to embrace civic engagement. Also, some staff who lead cocurricular activities are seeking advice in aligning them with the established civic engagement rubric. Our plan for the future is to add to our existing strategy by engaging every department in regular meaningful conversations about civic engagement and to formalize civic engagement professional development opportunities.

One next step we are exploring is to create a mechanism to certify faculty rather than courses to ensure the quality of civic engagement experiences. This idea has been submitted to a foundation for consideration, and we are currently looking for other funding sources. In the meantime, we are also working to extend the type of education and training we provide for full-time faculty and staff to those teaching part time. Adjuncts comprise approximately 40% of KCC's faculty, and part-timers teach a significant number of high-demand introductory certified CE courses, particularly on nights and weekends. We will need a process for educating adjunct faculty about KCC's civic engagement mission and supporting them in incorporating civic work into their classes if we are to ensure a meaningful experience for all our students. This is especially important as there is tremendous concern about ensuring the quality of the civic engagement experience in high-demand certified CE courses taught by part-timers. After KCC's experience with full-time faculty and staff, these concerns are not unwarranted. Much of our work going forward will focus on how to engage part-timers, and when and where such engagement is possible and necessary.

Conclusion

Higher education leaders are decrying the lack of civic engagement skills and awareness among college students. At the same time, the focus on graduation rates has pitted the need for civic learning against degree completion and workforce development, especially among community college students. The result is an inequity in the college experience between 2- and 4-year students. Upon the release of a 2012 report titled *A Crucible Moment: College Learning and Democracy's Future*, Dr. Carol Geary Schneider, president of the American Association of Colleges and Universities, commented: "It's not acceptable to have a two-tiered system in which some students are getting a full menu of preparation for a diverse democracy and global economy, but other students are getting narrow technical training" (Abdul-Alim, 2012, n.p.). She goes on to say that we shouldn't believe that the goal of 100% student engagement is too ambitious or unnecessary.

Kingsborough has demonstrated tremendous leadership and courage in remedying this inequity through its civic engagement graduation requirement. Despite the challenges we faced and are still facing, we are committed to giving 100% of our students the knowledge and skills needed to be an active participant in a democratic society. With community colleges educating nearly 50% of all undergraduates in the country, we hope that others follow our lead. We also hope that the challenges and lessons learned described in this report will help smooth the path for other institutions.

Reference

Abdul-Alim, J. (2012, January 10). Study: Two-thirds of college students surveyed say they lack civic engagement skills and awareness. Retrieved from http://www.citytowninfo.com/career-and-education-news/articles/political-engagement-among-college-students-at-all-time-low-12011202.

LAVITA MCMATH TURNER is director of government relations at Kingsborough Community College.

NEW DIRECTIONS FOR COMMUNITY COLLEGES • DOI: 10.1002/cc

7

This chapter describes fears that may lead to faculty resistance to civic engagement and suggests approaches to conquering these fears in order to further develop the civic capacities of our students and institutions.

Overcoming Faculty Fears About Civic Work: Reclaiming Higher Education's Civic Purpose

Cynthia Kaufman

De Anza College is a large regional community college located in the heart of the Silicon Valley. Our students are ethnically diverse and largely come from low-income backgrounds. De Anza has a reputation as an excellent transfer institution, so our students are on average highly motivated. Faculty and staff at De Anza have been working on equity and social justice agendas for many years, and the college's senior staff is committed to those goals. Our college president, Dr. Brian Murphy, is a cofounder of The Democracy Commitment, a national network of community colleges dedicated to achieving civic goals at our institutions.

For the past 3 years, I have been the director of De Anza's Institute of Community and Civic Engagement. The institute started as a focus group to see what kinds of civic engagement would fit with the culture of our campus and evolved into an office with a director and a small annual budget. My office has a number of successful projects, but few of them engage the faculty as a whole. This year I decided to reach out and encourage a broader range of faculty to engage in the work of developing the civic capacity of our students. This chapter describes the issues that arose in the process.

I began the project thinking that faculty already did a lot of civic work in their classes; they just didn't always know that they were doing it. Like many faculty members at De Anza and elsewhere, I have found that doing civic work in my own classes has been one of the more deeply rewarding aspects of my teaching. Thus, I assumed that with just a little bit of encouragement, I would find faculty ready to embrace the incorporation

NEW DIRECTIONS FOR COMMUNITY COLLEGES, no. 173, Spring 2016 © 2016 Wiley Periodicals, Inc.
Published online in Wiley Online Library (wileyonlinelibrary.com) • DOI: 10.1002/cc.20191

of civic practices into their classrooms. I assumed that I could facilitate this by helping them to see what they were already doing as civic and expanding on those strategies and activities. What I encountered, however, was a widespread and deeply rooted anxiety about stepping into the political, often seen as forbidden territory. After a brief description of how De Anza has worked over the past few years to develop the civic capacity of our students, this report describes the fears that I have come to see as the root of faculty resistance to civic engagement. I conclude with a few ways that my colleagues and I have worked toward conquering these fears in order to further develop the civic capacity of our students and our institutions.

The Move Toward Civic Skills at De Anza

In 2013 De Anza began to reexamine our core competency of "Global, Social, Cultural and Environmental Awareness." At the beginning of this process, many of us realized that the wording of the competency was very weak and that it needed to be redefined. In April 2013 the Institute began working with the director of equity, social justice, and multicultural education to develop a set of definitions for what faculty and staff were doing to increase the global, social, cultural, and environmental awareness of our students. What we realized during this process was that this core competency is inextricably intertwined with the civic skills and capacities of our students and indeed everyone on our campus. Thus, we recommended that the core competency be changed to "Civic Capacity for Equity, Sustainability, and Social Justice," a shift that has been embraced by the college's student learning outcomes team. We believe that having civic capacity for equity and social justice means that our students see themselves as active agents who have the skills and the motivation to bring about outcomes where people are treated with respect and empathy and where students are able to build a sustainable world in which people can realize their capacities.

Engaging Faculty in Developing Civic Competencies

As De Anza began to promote our redefined civic competency of Civic Capacity for Equity, Sustainability, and Social Justice, I began to engage faculty in conversations about what the competency means to them and how they would go about doing it. In particular, I began looking into the following questions:

- How can we encourage faculty to incorporate civic engagement when it is not a big part of what they do or teach?
- What kinds of trainings, invitations, or support result in faculty adopting some form of civic engagement into their classes?

- What language can be used to help faculty to see *what they are already doing* through the lens of civic engagement?
- What language can faculty use to help their *students* see what they are doing as civic engagement?

I believed that asking these questions would help De Anza better integrate a commitment to civic engagement into the college's culture. Therefore, I developed and piloted a short survey to assess how well faculty understood the concept of civic capacity and to ask them to identify ways they can work to develop the civic capacities of their students. I piloted the survey and led an in-depth discussion with a group of nine attendees at a workshop titled Developing Civic Capacity for Equity and Social Justice. What follows is a brief description of the survey results, as well as a larger exploration of some of the deeper and more useful findings from the workshop.

Survey Results.   Generally, faculty answered yes to almost all of the items I included in the survey as examples of things that would increase students' civic capacity. But very few of them said they were doing more than two or three of them. Thus, the issue was not about understanding the nature of civic capacity, but in taking on the work of developing students' civic capacity as one's own.

As noted previously, before administering the survey, I thought my main task would be to help people see the work they were already doing within the frame of civic capacity and that I would then use that frame to leverage more civic work and give faculty some tips on ways to integrate that work into their classes. I thought I would encounter resistance based on the worry that there isn't enough time to cover something more. The results were quite different. Almost all of the things that I had identified as civic were also agreed to as such by the participants in the survey. In other words, although not all of the faculty I surveyed employed all of the approaches to developing students' civic capacity, at least they understood that those approaches existed. Although I took some comfort from this, it left me asking why. If faculty are aware of these tactics for developing students' civic capacity, and they know doing so is an important part of our college's mission, why aren't they employing them?

The Root of Faculty Resistance: Fear

Although I learned a few things from the pilot administration of the survey, much more significant findings about the fears that faculty have about doing civic work emerged from our workshop conversations and from service learning training sessions. I quickly developed a strong sense that De Anza faculty—and likely those at other community colleges—believe that engaging students in civic work can be inappropriate or even dangerous. The fears I encountered fall into four categories: fear of abusing one's power as a faculty member, fear of being inappropriate, fear that civic discourse is

NEW DIRECTIONS FOR COMMUNITY COLLEGES • DOI: 10.1002/cc

dangerous in the classroom, and fear that civic discourse trains student to act in ways that will endanger them.

Fear 1: Engaging in Civic Discourse Imposes Our Values Inappropriately on Students.   One of the issues that surfaced repeatedly during conversations with faculty was the appropriateness of talking about politics in class. This view that politics and political opinions are inappropriate in the classroom appears to be quite widespread, even in political science classes, where faculty sometimes believe they must impart factual information and not engage in value-laden conversations. In my workshop, one faculty member said he'd love to talk about politics and civic issues but that he couldn't without it being an imposition of his power. This fear seems to be related to the view that an expression of an opinion is an *imposition* of one. This professor was sensitive to the power one holds as a faculty member and expressed a very sincere compassion for his students and a desire to not abuse that power.

Another poignant moment occurred when a different faculty member related that she always feels that students are looking to her for mentoring on what to think about important issues. She said she accepts this role except when it comes to controversial things like gay marriage. She then mused about what it might mean to go silent at precisely those moments when conversations are about issues of deep concern for students.

When I discuss this issue with colleagues, I hear many deeply felt worries about the importance of not proselytizing. So one question we need to wrestle with is where the boundaries are between proselyting and being present as engaged individuals. It seems to me that an important aspect of this is our own experience with mediating conversations across different points of view and our ability to hold open space for people whose views differ significantly from our own.

Fear 2: Engaging in Political or Electoral Discourse Is Illegal or Inappropriate.   The second fear expressed by many faculty at De Anza relates to the sense that it is illegal or inappropriate to discuss political or electoral issues in class or on campus. In 2012 there was a ballot initiative in the state of California to raise taxes. There was much at stake for higher education, as we were at the bottom of a multiyear budget crisis. The school was faced with a question of how to engage with the initiative. I asked one of our political science faculty members to write guidelines. In summary, these guidelines stated that as citizens of the state of California, it is essential for faculty to engage students about the importance of the election. It is illegal to tell student how to vote, but it is not illegal, or inappropriate, for faculty to talk about the factual implications of voting either way, or for the faculty member to express his or her own opinion.

These guidelines were presented to the faculty and staff on the first day of classes that year. Many of the faculty and staff worked hard to register students and to mobilize them to vote. We also informed students of what was at stake in the election. We did not tell them how to vote. Despite all these activities, there was much discomfort expressed on campus about faculty involvement in electoral issues, and many professors did not engage with the election at all. Still, many did, and the message from the administration that this form of political engagement was acceptable did seem relieving to many, who went on to talk to students about the election or to invite partisans to present on either side of the issue.

Fear 3: Teaching Our Students to Engage Civically Will Get Them into Trouble.   Another issue raised in the workshop was that if we help our students develop a civic voice they are likely to employ their voices in inappropriate places such as the workplace and get into trouble. Although we live in a nominally democratic society with constitutionally protected rights to free speech, within our culture are deep-seated prohibitions on engaging in civic discourse, especially in certain environments. The old adage that we should not talk about politics or religion is alive and well. It seems that many people in our society find civic discourse troubling and to be a source of conflict.

As we get students used to engaging in civic discourse, one of the things we need to do is teach them how to be smart about using their voices. Surely there are places and situations in which expression of political opinion is likely to elicit some negative responses. Students need to know that, and they need to learn to take risks intelligently. It seems that we need to teach not only civic skills, but strategy around when and where it is appropriate to use those skills, and to educate our faculty in ways of doing so.

Fear 4: Engaging in Civic Discourse Leads to Violence and Turmoil. A final issue raised in the civic engagement workshop essentially boils down to the fear that when people talk about politics, they inevitably get into fights. For example, one faculty member said she focused on providing only factual information in her classes—and never normative information—for fear that discussions of politics would lead to violence or at a minimum increased racial tensions or deeper divisions among student groups. We need to find ways to assuage faculty fears about this, provide professional development to help faculty feel more comfortable engaging their students in controversial issues, and put into place protections that will ensure that productive dialogues do not lead to nonproductive arguments or behaviors.

Internalized McCarthyism

As I learned more about faculty fears, I developed a profound respect for how devastated our public sphere is. Even at a college where the president and the senior staff openly support the need for civic discourse, faculty do not feel safe engaging in it. Reflecting on this, I realize that our campus actually offers little support for faculty in this regard. Recently, as students have begun to have more of a voice in campus political issues, I have been surprised how often their interventions—no matter how polite—are seen as inappropriate. Perhaps we have less of a democratic culture at my campus than I had realized. True, we often hold forums where controversial speakers come to speak, we put students in charge of a large budget, and the student government deliberates intensely on how to spend that money. We also have committees where faculty, staff, and managers deliberate in committee meetings about how to proceed in relation to various issues. Yet it is still quite rare to have serious issues deliberated publicly, and even rarer for students to be engaged in those deliberations. Why are we so afraid of civic discourse and of developing the civic capacities of our students? What can be done to combat faculty fears and, ideally, employ larger numbers of them in working toward a common goal of better preparing our students to live and work in a diverse democracy?

Upon reflection, I realized how long it has taken me to become comfortable with my role as a civic educator. Over the course of many years, I have worked though my thinking about this and debated it with many people. My own discipline is philosophy, with a specialization in social and political philosophy. I came to philosophy as a political activist and was appalled by the lack of engagement with real-world issues in my discipline. However, I was lucky enough to study in a program where faculty were engaged in a very explicit departmental struggle over the right for philosophy to be engaged. The book *Time in the Ditch: American Philosophy in the McCarthy Era* (McCumber, 2001) chronicles in great detail the shift in the discipline of philosophy from one of preparing people to be good citizens and moral agents to a very narrow concern with the analysis of language. McCumber argues that the transformation in the discipline was a direct result of a McCarthyist attack on academic philosophers who were social justice advocates. He shows how what began as an explicit political battle against the rights of left-wing philosophers to express their views came over the years to be accepted as normative behavior.

It seems that many people in the academic world have come to see their roles as imparters of neutral truths and not as coaches of living, social, human beings. My own perspective is that there is no such thing as neutrality. When we say we are neutral, we are usually manifesting the biases that are generally accepted within our community as normative. Furthermore, when faculty believe themselves to be neutral, they do not take responsibility for their positions and biases (conscious or un-). I have always let my students know that I have strong and unusual political views, that one of my political values is deep respect for the dignity of all people, and that a big part of my job is to open up space for people to explore who they are and what they believe in order to deepen those beliefs. This approach has worked well for me, and I find my classrooms to generally be places of open debate with diverse points of view being expressed. However, I now see that for those who do not have experience bringing their full civic selves into their work with students, the barriers to opening up civic space in the classroom are enormous.

New Directions for Community Colleges • DOI: 10.1002/cc

Conquering the Fears

The four fears I describe in this chapter are powerful, and they won't disappear overnight. Yet I believe that there are things we can and need to do to conquer these fears and play a positive role in developing the civic culture of our students:

- Our institutions need to model the democracy we wish our students to learn. Students need to see examples of people talking about real issues that have real consequences, and then see them coming away from these dialogues with mutual respect and safety.
- Faculty need to hear from administrators, in ways that are believable, that there is an expectation that we engage in civic dialogue and that we show our civic selves, full of opinions about real life issues and ready to engage opposing views with respect.
- We need to help develop in our students a sense of how to be strategic in their communication, when it is safe to be opinionated, when it is dangerous, and when those dangers are worth facing.
- We need to let faculty know the legal limits of political engagement in the classroom, not in order to chill their activity but to open up the space for all of the activities that fall short of that very narrow limit.
- We need to run our institutions in democratic ways, such that we teach democracy to our academic community by treating the places we work as microdemocracies in which people feel free to ask questions, challenge power, and deliberate productively.

One of the most productive questions I have found in my work with faculty on developing civic capacity is to ask them to reflect on the civic purposes of their discipline. We tend to fall into ruts and teach what we were taught so that students will succeed in school. When I asked faculty to think about the civic purpose of their discipline and the implications of this for their teaching, many responded that the question really challenged them to rethink what they were doing. For example, in my civic engagement workshop a professor in the hard sciences said that to her, science is a deep part of everything in the world. And yet, she hadn't thought about teaching science in ways that connect formulas and laws to broader civic themes. Similarly, we had a very lively discussion of math and the purposes of math and how wonderful it is to be in a class where math is put into the context of solving real problems, a class where students gain a sense of how they may end up using higher math in real life. How different a class like this is from simply being told a set of rules and being asked to apply them to equations.

To accomplish these objectives, we need to engage in serious staff development that asks faculty to reflect on their roles as civic educators. We need to help them to see themselves as engaged citizens and to see the development of a robust democracy as a part of their role as educators.

NEW DIRECTIONS FOR COMMUNITY COLLEGES • DOI: 10.1002/cc

Conclusion

If one of the purposes of higher education is to build the culture required to have a democratic society, we have a very long way to go. Higher education for many of us has been narrowed to a functionalist purpose. And yet, if our students don't learn how to be democratic citizens in college, where will they learn it? This brings to mind the admonition to parents that if they don't engage their children in conversations about sex, the knowledge their children acquire will be mostly what is found in commercial media. Similarly, if we don't teach civic skills, our students will learn from what they see in the media and in our capitalist culture. They will learn to avoid serious conversation; they will learn that those conversations are dangerous; and they will learn to remain silent.

Our society could be greatly enhanced by developing robust civic culture on our campuses and in our classrooms. We need campus administrators that give faculty explicit permission to engage; we need to provide faculty with the skills to open up conversations in ways that respect differences of opinion; we need to give faculty real experience negotiating differences in the microdemocracies that are our institutions. If we do this intentionally and explicitly, perhaps our colleges and universities can continue to be key sites for the strengthening of democracy.

Reference

McCumber, J. (2001). *Time in the ditch: American philosophy in the McCarthy era.* Chicago: Northwestern University Press.

CYNTHIA KAUFMAN *is director of the Institute of Community and Civic Engagement at De Anza College, California.*

8

This chapter describes a partnership between teacher education students at SUNY Broome and students at a local elementary school that led to all participants gaining a stronger sense of themselves as civic change agents in their communities.

Reframing Teacher Education for Democratic Engagement

Lisa Strahley, Tracy D'Arpino

Like most successful adventures, this one began with building strong relationships. Twenty-four fourth and fifth graders sat at tables around the library as the Public Achievement coaches (all students in a community college teacher education program) engaged them in a discussion about active listening. Each component of the Chinese symbol for listening—which includes the ears, the eyes, the mind, the heart, and undivided attention—became a focus. "I think they added the heart because sometimes it is important to feel what someone is saying," one student replied. Another added, "It's just polite and you might hear an idea you never thought of, which is good." Opportunities such as these to discuss effective ways to communicate and to listen to others' ideas helped the group build a foundation of acceptance. Through trainings received at State University of New York (SUNY) Broome Community College, the PA coaches understood that the students would be more open to risk taking and sharing ideas if they were comfortable with each other and shared a common goal.

The purpose of this chapter is to describe how a partnership between teacher education students at SUNY Broome and students at a local elementary school led to all participants' gaining a stronger sense of themselves as civic problem solvers and change agents in their communities. First, however, a little background.

Public schools have historically been stewards of democracy—places where our youth learn what it means to be informed participants in a democratic society. This occurs most often in high schools where students engage in civic-minded coursework, extracurricular activities, or service learning projects. Currently however, the academic landscape of public schools is

New Directions for Community Colleges, no. 173, Spring 2016 © 2016 Wiley Periodicals, Inc.
Published online in Wiley Online Library (wileyonlinelibrary.com) • DOI: 10.1002/cc.20192

undergoing such rapid change that there is a need not only to preserve but to contemporize and expand the way we instill civic capacity within our students. Classrooms—even in elementary schools—are the perfect learning laboratories to develop the knowledge and skills necessary for civic work. Public school teachers should be civic-minded role models for our youth and should be taught how to facilitate democratic engagement within the classroom.

Often in schools, teachers struggle with the student behaviors that they spend the least amount of time cultivating. These areas of frustration include a lack of ability to solve peer problems and a lack of understanding of how their behaviors affect others. Although curricular demands, pacing guides, and high-stakes testing might leave teachers feeling that there is little time to practice effective communication skills and civic behaviors with students, it may be that this work is necessary if students are to succeed in the classroom and in our democracy. As William Damon (2011) has stated, "The most serious danger Americans now face—greater than terrorism—is that our country's future may not end up in the hands of a citizenry capable of sustaining the liberty that has been America's most precious legacy. If trends continue, many young Americans will grow up without an understanding of the benefits, privileges, and duties of citizens in a free society, and without acquiring the habits of character needed to live responsibly in one" (p. 4). This begs the question, "In what ways can we engage our undergraduate teacher education students to be sufficiently equipped to facilitate opportunities to engage young students in civic work?"

Public Achievement at SUNY Broome

Typically, most college students practice some type of service learning during their education. Volunteer projects and service learning requirements are common on college campuses and serve to support various community needs. Civic engagement though, is a different approach. For example, providing support for a preestablished community cause is common with service learning projects. Civic engagement is different in that the participants act as change agents by selecting, researching, and resolving issues they perceive to be relevant in their community. In other words, rather than doing *for* the community, civic learning initiatives engage participates to become public actors or agents of democratic change *within* it.

Public Achievement, a youth civic engagement initiative, brings school-aged children (typically middle and high school) together to deliberate and act to address public issues of their choice. Coaches, usually college students, are trained in the Public Achievement curriculum and in turn are guided by coordinators, typically college professors. This training is usually embedded into the curriculum of a general education or elective course.

Although Public Achievement at SUNY Broome shares these characteristics, this initiative was different in two ways, in that we chose to emphasize

New Directions for Community Colleges • DOI: 10.1002/cc

civic learning in the teacher education program and to work with elementary school students. Traditionally, at this level teacher education programs focus heavily on instructional methods, philosophies, and classroom management. Yet as the program's instructors, we believed that infusing meaningful civic engagement and experiences into the curriculum would help future teachers develop in their students the skills necessary to flourish in a democratic society.

Thus, over two semesters in the 2013–14 academic year, 6 SUNY Broome teacher education students coached 24 elementary school students through the Public Achievement process and engaged them on a quest to resolve local issues. The children were invited to participate based on teacher recommendations, and all of them portrayed various civic-minded attributes. They were also representative of the district's racial, ethnic, and gender makeup. This after-school group met weekly with the SUNY Broome coaches for 18 weeks. Throughout the year, the locus of teaching was shifted from college professors to college students. Rather than receiving knowledge from an expert, learning was dynamic and was determined by the children's ideas and priorities. The coaches had to pose questions and facilitate student discussions to ensure that real-life problem solving occurred. All of the work was driven by genuine problems of concern identified by the elementary school students.

Initially, the school children had little knowledge about civic engagement but a great deal of enthusiasm. Early on, one was quoted as saying, "We can make a school lemonade stand and use the money to buy poor people shoes." Yet through the PA model, children learned the value of weighing options before jumping to conclusions. Brainstorming sessions, led by the coaches, helped students identify issues to investigate. Through a voting process, three issues emerged: supporting community health, decreasing school bullying, and getting involved in repairing the flooded school football field. Students formed three groups and began investigating the issues, eventually creating manageable action plans to work toward solutions.

Group A focused on supporting community health. Initially, the group researched a variety of factors that contribute to the health and well-being of the community. A challenge for the PA coaches was to help the students select a focal issue within this larger topic. As part of the research phase, the students interviewed the town mayor who stated that autism affected many of the families in the community. The children related to this, as they belong to a school district dedicated to the inclusion of all students and had several classmates with autism. Connecting with a teacher of autistic children, the group found that many autistic students have trouble communicating. The group then embarked on planning, publicizing, and holding an Autism Awareness fair at a local park to raise funds to purchase iPads for the teacher's classroom, with the aim of helping autistic students communicate more easily. The event was a huge success. A local singer entertained the crowd, gift baskets were raffled, and the children staffed games and face painting booths. The local state assemblywoman attended to the excitement of the students and, in the end, $800 was raised for iPads.

Group B focused on reducing school bullying. They interviewed the school's assistant principal and social worker. Through research they learned that bullying often happens because people don't understand each other. They then designed action plans to create a culture of caring within the school. The creation of a pen-pal program between students in grades 3 through 5 was the action plan that had the most influence on the children and the school environment. Interested students wrote weekly letters to an anonymous *new friend* to help students better understand each other. This project soon caught on and the PA students began collecting and delivering mail for 20 participating partners. The project concluded with a reveal party and celebration for improving the school culture.

Group C put their efforts toward investigating the process to repair the district's football field in hopes they could be a part of the development. A flood had damaged the structures and property, rendering the field unusable. This investigative work was difficult and required patience from the students and their coaches. They interviewed school business officials and wrote letters to Federal Emergency Management Agency representatives. Responses were scarce and were not received for weeks. These roadblocks hindered the anticipated progress of the group but also taught them valuable lessons in perseverance. The children decided to adjust and focused their efforts toward creating a new field design and researching the cost of the desired items. Although their progress was slow, the children learned to look at a problem from many angles to achieve a resolution.

PA coaches were imperative to the success of these three action projects. For 30 minutes after each class, the coaches met to debrief and create lesson plans for the next meetings. They established a protocol in which the children had to reflect on their progress and use the PA cycle to plan for next steps. Coaches learned how to facilitate conversation around an important topic, to foster inquiry skills over immediate action, and to allow the children to hear various viewpoints. They also were able to keep the children focused on their action plans and to provide next-step support so the projects came to fruition.

Results of the Initiative

In an effort to measure the success of the initiative, pre- and postsurveys were administered to both undergraduate teacher education students and the young learners. The surveys focused on attitudes, behaviors, and knowledge of democratic civic practices. The data showed a positive shift toward greater civic responsibility and action for both respondent groups. Some significant changes included attributes, such as "I feel it is important to understand different perspectives when trying to solve problems," "I am

NEW DIRECTIONS FOR COMMUNITY COLLEGES • DOI: 10.1002/cc

aware of effective strategies for solving local issues," and "I actively engage in community work to help address local issues."

Furthermore, the future teachers (PA coaches) also indicated that they felt more responsibility to work to resolve community issues. The experience altered their perspectives on being change agents within a community and showed them the importance of engaging youth in civic work. Furthermore, the coaches all agreed that this was the hardest yet most meaningful aspect of what they had learned and practiced that school year. All commented positively on the valuable skills they could apply to their future professional careers, and half of them noted that they would continue with the project, even though they would no longer receive course credit.

The young students also gained communication and leadership skills. They took risks that would not have been afforded to them without the support of the PA coaches. For example, each student called adults on the phone to set up interviews, wrote letters to government officials, planned with school personnel, or spoke to parents and local news reporters. The value of active involvement in a problem-solving process cultivated skills in these young children that will last a lifetime.

Lessons Learned

We highly encourage teacher education programs to create courses that teach preservice teachers a process for civic learning and democratic engagement and to allow sufficient time (we used two semesters) for community college students to learn, design, and implement the PA curriculum and for meaningful learning to take place. The PA model provided direct opportunities for coaches to improve communication skills and to work as a team to create and implement lesson plans. Weekly reflection also allowed the participants to self-assess and adjust plans. Problems were generated from the school-aged children's daily concerns, issues they were passionate about. This recipe fostered an environment of high energy, frequent risk taking, and dynamic teamwork. These are skills desired by all candidates graduating from a teacher preparation program.

The outcomes of this project were inspirational. PA coaches were asked to develop and foster skills that are often undervalued in today's schools and did so with success. The young students gained a strong sense of themselves as civic problem solvers and change agents in their community. Through the PA curriculum, children were able to learn a process for problem solving. When roadblocks occurred, students revisited prior action plans and made adjustments to better suit their desired outcomes. The power of the student voice led to a rich, authentic experience. This engagement, which was rooted in their community and experiences, fostered important skills and, perhaps more important, a sense of civic responsibility.

A central focus of our program was to help community college teacher education students develop skills to use in the classroom and in a democratic society. An added outcome was the empowerment of students (both college and school aged) to learn that agency resides in the people. This experience increased the civic-mindedness of all participants and led to authentic, unforgettable learning.

In a series of papers titled "School and Society," John Dewey (1915) wrote: "Democracy has to be born anew in every generation, and education is its midwife" (p. 15). The unique endeavor piloted by SUNY Broome lays the foundation for undergraduate teacher education students to become facilitators of civic work, gaining the knowledge and tools needed to educate the whole child in an era of 21st century demands.

References

Damon, W. (2011). *Failing liberty 101: How we are leaving young Americans unprepared for citizenship in a free society.* Palo Alto, CA: Hoover Institution Press.
Dewey, J. (1915). *School and society.* Chicago: University of Chicago Press.

LISA STRAHLEY is chair of the Early Childhood and Teacher Education Department and coordinator of the Civic Engagement Center at SUNY Broome Community College.

TRACY D'ARPINO is assistant principal at Johnson City Central Schools.

9

This chapter describes a diversity and democracy curriculum and faculty development collaboration among the Association of American Colleges and Universities, The Democracy Commitment, and 10 community colleges.

Bridging Cultures to Form a Nation: The Humanities and Democratic Learning

Caryn McTighe Musil

As I grew up, there's change in the neighborhood
From respectable citizens to "Boys in the Hood"
Adult or thug were the choices for me
What has happened to my Community?

I have grown up, I'm an adult now
I'll strive to give voice somewhere, some how
I am in college, this semester I have learnt a lot
With my Community and Civic Engagement so I'll give it a shot

The act of a citizen is to be involved in affairs
An active citizen is one who cares
He is concerned about problems of the neighborhood
And tries to go about encouraging others to do good.

These lines are part of a longer poem by Shamar Brooks, a Kingsborough Community College student in New York City (Kingsborough Community College, 2015, p. 1). They demonstrate that students are yearning for ways that colleges can help them make sense of their lives and empower them with knowledge and skills so that they can create a better world. Fortunately for Shamar, he went to a college that believes its civic mission is integral—not ancillary—to its educational one. Kingsborough was 1 of 10 community colleges selected to be part of a 3-year project called *Bridging Cultures to Form a Nation: Difference, Community, and Democratic Thinking.* This project, funded by the National Endowment for the Humanities (NEH) and organized jointly by the Association of American Colleges and Universities (AAC&U) and The Democracy Commitment (TDC), involved 10

NEW DIRECTIONS FOR COMMUNITY COLLEGES, no. 173, Spring 2016 © 2016 Wiley Periodicals, Inc.
Published online in Wiley Online Library (wileyonlinelibrary.com) • DOI: 10.1002/cc.20193

community colleges from across the nation: Chandler-Gilbert Community College (AZ), County College of Morris (NJ), Georgia Perimeter College (GA), Kapi'olani Community College (HI), Kingsborough Community College (NY), Lone Star College-Kingwood (TX), Miami Dade College (FL), Middlesex Community College (MA), Mount Wachusett Community College (MA), and Santa Fe College (FL). As the key author and initial project director of the grant, I have had the pleasure of working with the community college teams over the 3 years of the project and witnessing their innovative, creative, and committed work.

Bridging Cultures to Form a Nation represents an emphatic statement from AAC&U and TDC that community colleges are important sites for educating students for engaged participation and leadership in a diverse democracy, as well as for the global citizenship necessary in our deeply contentious, interdependent world. Furthermore, *Bridging Cultures* served as a catalyst for supporting a critical mass of faculty and staff—despite limited resources and time and, for some, adjunct status—in creating more opportunities for students to deepen their civic skills, knowledge, and commitment. The project aimed to put more students in classrooms that intentionally fostered democratic dispositions and knowledge as part of the academic rigor of the course.

The Civic Origins of the Project

Bridging Cultures to Form a Nation was conceived in 2011 in a climate (which still persists) where some leaders are trying to shrink the purposes of all colleges to narrowly focused and simplistically conceived vocational ends. Using the language of workforce development, many advocate simply matching the curriculum to a given state's current job openings. Yet doing so ignores what business leaders say about preparation for a fluid, technology-laden, knowledge-driven, fast-paced work world. Employers from for-profits and nonprofits alike tell researchers that it is more important for students to have a broad grounding in liberal arts and sciences than specialized training (Hart Research Associates, 2013). Further, a one-note understanding of the purposes of higher education is dangerous and pushes any education for democratic life entirely off the table.

Despite a pervasive, single-minded focus on community colleges solely as sites of industry training—which both marginalizes the humanities as disciplines and the historic public purpose of community college—TDC's goal is that "every graduate of an American community college shall have had an education in democracy. This includes all of our students, whether they aim to transfer to university, achieve an associate degree or obtain a certificate" (The Democracy Commitment, 2015, n.p.). Similarly, AAC&U argues that students' education must be anchored through active involvement with diverse communities as they tackle together issues of public concern.

The Purpose and Design of Bridging Cultures to Form a Nation

In light of the public mission of higher education, community colleges and other institutions must grapple with how to define the capabilities students need to be effective citizens in their communities or at work. As institutions began to embed opportunities for civic learning into their curricula and pedagogy, *Bridging Cultures* sought to address these challenging questions head on through three principal goals: (a) to infuse questions about difference, community, and democratic thinking into high-enrollment transfer humanities courses; (b) to promote greater adoption of proven high-impact practices linked to retention and academic achievement; and (c) to create over a 3-year period a series of humanities-enriched professional development opportunities for community college faculty, including adjuncts. The key to the *Bridging Cultures* project is its support for faculty professional development in order to transform high-enrollment humanities transfer courses. External support was available for travel, meetings, a 5-day summer institute, campus-based forums, and faculty minigrants. Through these and other strategies, colleges were able to refine, initiate, or invest in education for democracy projects on their campuses. Most of the institutions also collaborated with student affairs professionals to complement and reinforce what was being learned in the classroom.

The Humanities and Civic Capacities.   Because NEH was the funder, *Bridging Cultures* was able to underscore how critical the humanities disciplines are in our diverse democracy and how they can provide a space of engagement in the midst of a wrangling and divisive world. The project asserts that when humanities courses are structured around difference, community, and democratic thinking, they can illuminate how it has been and can be possible to bridge the divides apparent in the nation and to realize the democratic ideal of E Pluribus Unum. Through civically enriched courses, students can begin to acquire a set of critical democratic capacities to navigate the complexities they routinely confront. We believe such courses also encourage them to engage across differences. A democracy cannot flourish and, in the extreme, cannot function, if its people lack either the will or the ability to engage thoughtfully and responsibly with others in the public sphere. Steeped in the practice of entering imaginatively into other people's lives and worldviews, the humanities serve as "sources of national memory and civic vigor, cultural understanding and communication, individual fulfilment and the ideals we hold in common" (Commission on the Humanities and Higher Education, 2013, p. 9).

Indeed, rather than being an abstraction or a luxury, the humanities plunge students into the very midst of the world's dilemmas and crises over time. They immerse students in the lives of total strangers through literature and history, anthropology and foreign languages, and through that immersion turn what is unfamiliar into a shared stage of human activity. Nussbaum (2010) elucidates the process of connecting one's imagination with real-world democratic decision making, thus underscoring the civic mission of humanities within community colleges:

> We need the imaginative ability to put ourselves in the position of people different from ourselves, whether by class or race or religion or gender. Democratic politics involves making decisions that affect other people and groups. We can only do this well if we try to imagine what their lives are like and how changes of various sorts affect them. The imagination is an innate gift, but it needs refinement and cultivation: this is what the humanities provide. (para. 6)

The Bridging Cultures Summer Institute. The *Bridging Cultures* project was launched in 2012 with a 5-day residential summer institute at the University of Vermont at which some 60 faculty members and administrators from the 10 community colleges could explore more deeply the project's themes of difference, community, and democratic thinking. At the intellectual heart of the summer institute were its four topical seminars where groups of 12–15 people from different schools met each day for 2½ hours to discuss the readings and their implications for course redesigns. The first seminar, E Pluribus Unum: Democracy's Tensions and Higher Education's Civic Mission, explored foundational values that animate democratic nations around the globe (including the United States) and the persistent question of which people get to claim those values. The second seminar, Bridging Cultures: Immigration, Nationalism, and E Pluribus Unum, explored the understanding of citizenship and belonging, and the relationship between national and cultural identity for immigrant groups over time. In the third seminar, Religious Pluralism in a Democratic Global Age, readings investigated how religious freedom, a hallmark of liberal democracy, is undermined by religious intolerance, discrimination, and violence. Finally, the fourth seminar, Movement for Public Voice and Democratic Engagement, went to the heart of democratic struggles for social justice as diverse communities sought fuller inclusion, voice, and rights in the American experiment.

No one was an expert in all the readings nor did people agree in their interpretations or responses. So we all quickly became students— uncertain, tentative, inquiring, vulnerable, and sometimes emotional in our exchanges. We had to stretch ourselves to create spaces of democratic engagement together just as we hoped to do in *Bridging Cultures* humanities courses. We understood in the seminars that a classroom is a treasured space both to study *about* democracy and to practice *doing* democracy. The institute also included colloquia with humanities scholars, poster sessions led by the 10 teams, time for institutional planning, consultancies with a national advisory group, and practical workshops on all sorts of topics from democratic pedagogies, to navigating differences, to incorporating community-based experiences into teaching, to assessing student learning.

Teams returned home from the summer institute to initiate professional development opportunities so that they could expand the number of professors ready to rethink their courses. Some immediately began to infuse *Bridging Cultures* themes across humanities courses or in some cases invent entirely new courses. As their work progressed, many members presented their *Bridging Cultures* work at AAC&U conferences, disciplinary conferences, and to colleagues on their home campuses. A number published articles on their progress. Many were part of ongoing faculty study groups. Almost all colleges worked with their teaching and learning center or their center for civic engagement (if they had one), and most could point to resource banks they had developed during the course of the project. All invested in creating dynamic classroom experiences for their students.

It must be noted that the 10 community colleges did not enter the project as civic novices. They were in it because they had already achieved national recognition for their leadership in advancing civic learning and democratic engagement. Nine of the 10 schools were inaugural members of The Democracy Commitment. Some of the most eloquent voices championing the civic mission of community colleges were presidents and top academic administrators from *Bridging Cultures* schools, who were backed by faculty with similar commitments. In part because of their existing commitments to education for citizenship, what these 10 colleges were able to accomplish in 3 years is inspiring.

Democratic Education in Action: Curricular Innovations

The most remarkable accomplishments of the *Bridging Cultures* project were in curriculum transformation and faculty development. By the numbers alone, the scope of the project's curricular reach was stunning. Kingsborough estimates that 130 sections were offered under the *Bridging Cultures* grant, exposing 3,250 students to themes of diversity, community-building, and democratic thinking. County College of Morris believes they reached 1,450 students through revised curricula and an impressive 400 faculty attended faculty professional development events. The latter, of course, is a predictor that even more courses are likely to be revised in the coming years. In 2 years Miami Dade revised 84 class sections and reached over 3,200 students, and Mount Wachusett revised 54 courses reaching 939 students. Middlesex reported that 21 courses (some 60 sections) had been redesigned, reaching 1,700 students. At Lone Star-Kingwood, the project grew from an initial team of 6 to 50 faculty, thus reaching thousands of students each semester.

Cumulatively, every humanities discipline was involved and because of the excitement about the project, faculty from courses beyond the humanities began to transform their courses too. According to Lone Star-Kingwood's final report (2015), "by the end of the first year, faculty from every academic division on this campus of 12,000 students were represented in the work" (p. 3). The most common way courses were transformed was by introducing rich and sometimes unsettling themes into regular course content. Additional learning was derived through the civic-oriented pedagogies that professors adopted or refined. The following sections illustrate specific changes made in various disciplines.

English.   In both his writing and literature courses, an English professor at Kingsborough introduced themes of inequality, identity, and ethics. His students investigated how one's ethics influences how one acts. The professor also designed assignments for hands-on work at multiple sites. Students volunteered at the New York Asian Women's Center to address the consequences of human trafficking, organized events about modern forms of slavery, held debates at Kingsborough's Eco-festival, or worked at the Urban Farm. Another Kingsborough English professor examined themes of gender identity, racism, and religious tolerance in Shakespeare's plays by asking students to produce a play that had modern resonance. One student changed the setting of *The Merchant of Venice* to the 1940s when Pakistan was created out of India, leading to massive violence by Hindus against Muslims. Another student opted to set *Twelfth Night* in 1980s New York City at the start of the AIDS epidemic. At Santa Fe College, an American Humanities course was redesigned to include assignments in which students explored their own immigration story and compared it with those of other groups.

History.   In a Twentieth Century American History class at County College of Morris, a history professor invited analysis of civic duties and democratic practices during the Great Depression. For their capstone assignment in the course, students conducted group research highlighting democracy in action as it was recorded in local newspapers. One of Kingsborough's modern history classes lifted up themes of social movements for equality such as the civil rights movement, United Farm Workers Union, and the women's movement. Documentary films became integral to the class, including the Japanese "The Cats of Mirikitani," which touched on the bombing of Hiroshima, Japanese Internment camps, and 9/11. Santa Fe College remapped its U.S. history course to 1877 to highlight the interconnectedness of the Atlantic world. Professors asked students to research the experience of Africans as forced immigrants and Europeans as voluntary immigrants. Students could opt to write a first-person narrative about either one of the two, or they could examine their own position on the current debate over immigrants and immigration.

Similarly, history classes at Lone Star-Kingwood are deemphasizing the nation–state as the best way to organize history and instead exploring transnational perspectives that underscore global interconnections. They are also emphasizing how history is constructed, revealing how power influences what versions of history are disseminated. By highlighting history from below and including the study of ordinary people, the *Bridging Cultures* historians at Lone Star-Kingwood are seeking to "empower our students to perceive themselves as the makers of their own history" (2015, p. 3). Their History 2301 course includes content on immigrant experiences matched with hands-on experiences with border cultures, enhanced through oral histories, service learning, and research projects. Although not a history course, County College of Morris' Spanish I class also drew upon the richness of the institution's immigrant communities and challenged students to think more inclusively about local Hispanic residents and recognize the rich diversity within Spanish-speaking countries.

Communication.   The County College of Morris infused themes of diversity, community, and democracy into its Introduction to Film class, using documentaries as mechanisms to foster awareness of social issues and to encourage democratic participation. At Lone Star-Kingwood, students in an Intro to Communications class were paired with students in English as a Second Language (ESOL) classes to deepen intercultural understanding through collaborative projects. ESOL students introduced communication students to new countries and cultures, and communication students helped ESOL students with their oral and written communication skills.

Philosophy.   Two philosophy courses at Mount Wachusett, one of which is the required capstone for all liberal arts and science majors, were revamped to include issues of race and class in the Philosophy of Self and Ethics Modules, along with questioning how definitions of democracy, freedom, and justice are constructed. An ethics course at Santa Fe incorporated an experiential learning component through which students engaged in a community-based experience and then wrote a reflective paper tying their experience to an ethical concept in the course.

Photography and Art.   Several Miami Dade art professors sought to open deliberations across campuses by bringing student art out of the classroom into more public spaces. They also incorporated notions of civic action into their subject matter. One professor stressed what he called Creating Artivists, that is, artist citizen activists. In an art appreciation course, students were asked to create art around a social issue to generate awareness. This led one student to create an art piece on sex trafficking and another to use recycled materials to create a piece on saving the environment. In a somewhat similar mode of using art to engage in public issues, a photography class at Mount Wachusett required students to visually represent their interpretation of democracy—and they were forbidden to use monuments or flags. Student work was then showcased in campus galleries and display cases to prompt a wider dialogue.

Learning Communities.   Several campuses constructed *Bridging Cultures* learning communities, high-impact practices connected to improved learning, retention, and expanding intercultural skills and knowledge about diversity. Chandler Gilbert created a new first-year experience learning community with *Bridging Cultures* as the organizing theme and an interdisciplinary focus on history, composition, philosophy, environmental ethics, and women's studies. Similarly, Kapi'olani created a learning community called "Ho'I ou I ke Po'owai: A Return to the Water Source" that involved courses in Hawaiian art, environmental philosophy, and public speaking.

The Professoriate as Citizen Activists

One of the most intriguing revelations evident in the *Bridging Cultures* project final reports was how faculty were actually functioning as engaged citizens on their own campuses. They understood the deep democratic power of community colleges and therefore almost all of the teams organized strategically, creatively, and collectively to persuade others to tap this resource more intentionally. Their campus became their public square. They organized, reached out to a broad range of faculty, and made sure they included adjuncts, even if they were the lowest paid, most transient, and most vulnerable colleagues. They invested in educating others about the themes of democracy they found most compelling, offered workshops, created public symposiums and forums, and designed citywide or regional conferences to bring new people to the table. Faculty reached for allies first outside of their disciplinary domain and then through student affairs colleagues, students themselves, public intellectuals and artists, and community-based organizations with whom they established stronger partnerships. They took time to create mechanisms for more intimate dialogues and study, told personal stories, and listened while others told theirs.

They also assessed their current institutional structures and sought to make them more functional, inclusive, and effective. Some redesigned their general education courses, introduced more democratic pedagogies, established a new two-part civic engagement requirement for every student (Kingsborough), or worked to advance a new statewide civic learning outcome (Middlesex). Mount Wachusett created an Endowed Chair of Civic Engagement, a new full-time faculty position that will help anchor and expand future civic work. Like all good democratic cultures, the *Bridging Cultures* teams relied on dispersed leadership that shared a common commitment to deploying community colleges as sites for democratic learning and action.

This chapter began with a poem by Kingsborough student Shamar Brooks who discovered at college the power he possessed as a citizen who is responsible for and committed to improving his community. Over the 3 years of the *Bridging Cultures* project, the ever-expanding numbers of faculty involved affirmed a similar power to be citizens at their community colleges, making the institution more responsive to the needs of their students, their local communities, the nation, and the globe. As John Dethloff (2014) from Lone Star-Kingwood put it so eloquently, "Classrooms should serve not only as meeting places for students or training grounds for future employees; they should provide a space for the birth of citizens" (p. 18).

References

Commission on the Humanities and Higher Education. (2013). *The heart of the matter: The humanities and social sciences for a vibrant, competitive, and secure nation.* Cambridge, MA: American Academy of Arts and Sciences.

Dethloff, J. (2014). Bridging cultures to form a nation: A project for democracy. *Diversity & Democracy, 17*(3), 18–19.

Hart Research Associates. (2013). It takes more than a major: Employer priorities for college learning and student success. *Liberal Education, 99*(2), 22–29.

Kingsborough Community College. (2015). *Bridging cultures to form a nation final report.* Washington, DC: Association of American Colleges and Universities.

Lone Star College-Kingwood. (2015). *Bridging cultures to form a nation final report.* Washington, DC: Association of American Colleges and Universities.

Nussbaum, M. (2010, October 17). Cultivating the imagination. *New York Times* (online ed.). Retrieved from http://www.nytimes.com/roomfordebate/2010/10/17/do-colleges-need-french-departments/cultivating-the-imagination.

The Democracy Commitment. (2015). *About us.* Washington, DC: Author. Retrieved rom http://thedemocracycommitment.org/.

CARYN MCTIGHE MUSIL *is senior scholar and director of civic learning and democracy initiatives at the Association of American Colleges and Universities.*

NEW DIRECTIONS FOR COMMUNITY COLLEGES • DOI: 10.1002/cc

10

This chapter describes the cocurricular activities offered through The Democracy Commitment at Allegany College of Maryland and the impact of these civic experiences on its students.

Civic Engagement at a Small Rural College: If We Can Do It…

Kurt Hoffman

Much has been written documenting the potential of community colleges to act as the center of community development and the resurrection of economic life in rural communities (e.g., Eddy, 2007; Emory & Flora, 2006). In rural areas, schools tend to be imbedded in their communities and provide a cultural hub and sense of place for local residents. Because of the interdependent relationship between rural schools and communities, an investment in one invariably leads to the improvement of the other; a thriving community results in an increase in the tax base, which benefits schools, just as thriving colleges provide an economic draw in terms of new citizens, a more educated populace, and businesses looking to relocate. One way in which campuses and communities can be further integrated is through the experiential processes of civic engagement. Civic engagement allows curricula and community to merge; these activities provide authentic learning experiences that address issues facing the community by connecting them with lessons taught in the classroom.

Unfortunately, rural colleges tend to lack institutional capacity for civic engagement, at least in comparison with their urban counterparts. Rural colleges tend to be smaller and less well funded. They often rely on AmeriCorps volunteers or faculty champions to initiate and maintain civic programs and are less likely to have funded and institutionalized centers for civic engagement. Furthermore, the lack of resources may cause civic engagement to be seen as less of an institutional priority, and the laserlike focus on degree completion and job preparation can make civic engagement feel like a liberal education luxury.

NEW DIRECTIONS FOR COMMUNITY COLLEGES, no. 173, Spring 2016 © 2016 Wiley Periodicals, Inc.
Published online in Wiley Online Library (wileyonlinelibrary.com) • DOI: 10.1002/cc.20194

Even though community colleges have possessed a dual public mission—a civic mission devoted to educating students for participation in democracy and an economic one in which students are prepared for their future vocations—the economic mission has come to dominate the community college agenda. As Stoeker & Schmidt (2008) state: "To the extent that service learning can add to the problem-solving capacity of excluded and oppressed communities, rural communities are once again left at the back of the line in accessing needed services" (p. 10). And should a program be fortunate enough to secure either internal or external funding, the ongoing problem will be to maintain and commit to it in the future, as institutional priorities will inevitably shift. It is within this complicated context that Allegany College of Maryland (ACM) finds its fledgling civic engagement work.

The Democracy Commitment at Allegany College of Maryland

ACM is a small rural community college located at the foothills of the Appalachian Mountains in western Maryland, a metro area that has experienced a 50% population decrease since the 1950s and designated by various media outlets as one of the top 10 poorest cities in the country. Founded in 1961, ACM enrolls 3,500 students; 44% of these are the first in their families to attend college. Over 80% are financial aid recipients.

In 2011 ACM became one of the original signatories of the newly formed The Democracy Commitment (TDC), a national consortium supporting the civic work of community colleges, and soon thereafter the college invited faculty and staff to join a steering committee that would ultimately guide the civic engagement work at the college—10 professors and the Student Government Association staff director volunteered. The idea was strategic: By forming a committee, TDC at ACM would not be dependent upon a faculty champion, and the work of instituting civic engagement programs and activities would not fall on any single person. The steering committee was designed to operate democratically with all voices and perspectives welcome in the decision-making process. I function as the lead of the steering committee and the official TDC campus coordinator, responsible for creating agendas, facilitating meetings, collecting summary programming information, and liaising with the national TDC.

The first committee meetings involved a fair bit of research and discussion of the literature regarding civic engagement, including the various ways of defining it. The committee was reassured to learn that TDC—at a national level—was also struggling with this issue. At this point, the ACM steering committee determined that their work should proceed along two lines: increasing the committee's understanding of civic engagement and simultaneously offering civic and democratic cocurricular programming to students, the community, faculty, and staff. The steering committee decided to focus its civic work on cocurricular presentations, as it knew from previous experience that they could be an effective way to engage ACM students in social and political issues. As well, cocurricular programming was strategically chosen because the steering committee felt it would not be subject to political resistance from any constituent groups on campus; the programs were accomplishable and therefore possessed a likelihood of success, and the work could be kept within the group by drawing upon the expertise of various members of the committee. Although the committee liked the idea of a curricular civic pathway at ACM, we knew that particular track was premature and would likely face resistance. The goal became to offer cocurricular presentations that would incrementally introduce issues leading to greater civic engagement among students. Through these civic engagement activities, students would increase their civic agency; in other words, increase their capacity to act collaboratively and cooperatively on common problems and challenges. The steering committee believed that as students engaged in more civic activities and as their civic empowerment increased, the institution's civic capacity to support these activities would also grow. The steering committee's ultimate vision was and is to create a civic culture that permeates all layers of the college, allowing a civic curriculum across multiple disciplines to emerge.

Investigating the Impact of Cocurricular Civic Presentations

An abundance of research demonstrates the benefits of civic engagement activities on academic engagement and achievement, retention and persistence, completion and degree attainment, critical thinking, writing, communication, and interpersonal effectiveness (e.g., Finlay, 2011; Gallini & Moely, 2003; Vogelsang & Astin, 2005). Yet few studies specifically examine civic engagement at rural institutions (Holton, 2009; Stoecker & Schmidt, 2008), and research examining the effects of one-time cocurricular presentations on students' civic attitudes and civic behaviors is much less common than that assessing the self-reported outcomes of course- or community-based civic programs (Hoy & Meisel, 2008; Keen & Hall, 2009).

In this study, I set out to investigate the outcomes of TDC cocurricular programming at ACM. More specifically, the purpose of this mixed-design project was to investigate student and faculty perceptions of the college's civic engagement activities and to assess whether the cocurricular activities led to greater civic engagement among attendees. Specifically, I asked the following questions:

1. Does attending one or more TDC cocurricular activities have an effect on participants' self–reported civic attitudes and behaviors, political engagement, and/or global awareness and understanding, and more specifically, do the effects differ by number of activities attended?
2. Does the *type* of cocurricular presentation affect participants' responses?

New Directions for Community Colleges • DOI: 10.1002/cc

To investigate these questions, I developed and administered a survey consisting of 20 questions, 7 of which I developed and 13 were adapted from the Student Community Engagement Scale from Indiana University-Purdue University Indianapolis and from the California Civic Index. In addition to three questions asking about the respondents' age and gender, as well as whether they are a student, faculty, or staff member, the remaining questions linked to four content areas: civic attitudes, civic behaviors, global understanding, and political engagement. These questions were attitudinal measures and were divided into two Likert-type scales: a "likelihood" scale that asks respondents how likely they were to do something, and an "agreement" scale that asked them how much they agreed with each statement. The survey was administered to 244 students, faculty, staff, and community members in a variety of modalities in order to increase the response rate. All data were coded by date and event. Acting as a participant observer, I also collected additional qualitative data in order to provide greater contextual understanding of the events.

I administered the survey 12 times in fall 2013 following various cocurricular events. The first TDC at ACM activity was called Clergy Beyond Borders: Caravan of Reconciliation. This event was presented by an evangelical Methodist minister, a rabbi, a Lutheran minister, and a Muslim imam. The group's stated goal was to create an event with "multifaith participation to highlight a statewide commitment to pluralism and diversity in order to prevent interreligious and racial conflict." There were 22 faculty, students, and staff in attendance, and 10 responded to the postpresentation survey.

The second activity was organized by the student-led Peace Studies Club and centered around *A Place at the Table*, an award-winning documentary about hunger in America. Student members of the Peace Studies Club introduced the movie, framed the issue, offered local statistics to demonstrate the situation within the community, and invited local food pantries to talk briefly about their work in the community. Roughly 175 attended two showings of the movie, and 88 responded to the postpresentation survey.

Finally, TDC at ACM held 10 Campus Conversations—deliberative dialogues on the theme of race and ethnicity. Deliberative dialogues are an approach to civic and democratic engagement designed by the Kettering Foundation and used in its National Issues Forums. These hour-long dialogues were conducted in various rooms across campus and at numerous times over the semester. They had such large attendance that more conversations were scheduled, and additional sessions were facilitated for entire classes during their regularly scheduled-meeting times. A total of 247 students, faculty, and staff participated in these dialogues, and 146 filled out the survey. Across all three types of activities, response rates ranged from 45% to 59%, for an aggregate response rate of 55%.

NEW DIRECTIONS FOR COMMUNITY COLLEGES • DOI: 10.1002/cc

Analysis and Results

The primary purpose of this investigation was to examine the effect of attending one or more TDC at ACM events on attendees' civic attitudes, civic behaviors, global understanding, and political engagement, and specifically to test whether the effects differed by the number of presentations attended or by presentation type.

Does Repeated Exposure to Civic Opportunities Matter?   To address the first question—do the effects of cocurricular civic presentations differ by the number of events attended—respondents were grouped into three categories based on the total number of TDC at ACM events in which they participated: 1 (this was their first event), 2 (this was the second time they participated in a TDC event), and 3+ (this was at least their third TDC presentation). A comparison of the means of the three attendance groups for each of the 17 content-related survey questions was completed to determine if the differences were statistically significant. Of the 17 questions, 3 showed statistically significant differences of either $(\alpha = .10)$, $(\alpha = .05)$ or $(\alpha = .01)$ among the three attendance groups. The significance levels reflect the probability that the measured differences between the groups could be due to random chance: an $\alpha = .10$ means that we have 90% confidence that the differences measured were related to the number a civic events attended and *not* to chance. Similarly, confidence levels of $\alpha = .05$ and $\alpha = .01$ means that we can be 95% and 99% sure, respectively, that the differences were due to attendance at civic events. These three survey questions represented three of the four areas of civic engagement: civic behavior, political engagement, and global understanding. No questions in the area of civic attitude possessed a statistical difference, and none of the other 14 questions showed statistically significant differences among the groups.

Based on my analysis, the desire to work with others to "solve a problem in the community" appears to increase depending on the number of civic cocurricular presentations attended. Indeed, there was a statistically significant difference between the mean scores of respondents who were attending a TDC at ACM event for the first time and those who had attended three or more events. In other words, the more civic presentations attended, the more likely respondents were to agree they would work to solve problems in their community.

As well, respondents who had attended three or more events were statistically more likely than those attending only one to indicate that they would "sign an email or paper petition related to the issue presented," although this effect was not significant among groups that had attended either two or three + presentations. This indicates that three or more exposures to civic cocurricular presentations may be necessary to inspire greater political engagement among students, faculty, and staff.

The last question that showed statistically significant differences between the three groups dealt with respondents' sense of global understanding and engagement. Specifically, attendees of three or more TDC events were more likely than those who attended only two presentations (who were in turn more likely than those who attended only one) to agree that "I have a responsibility to use the knowledge I gained today to address global issues." In other words, each successive event led to an increase in attendees' desire to address global issues.

These findings are particularly relevant to civic educators at ACM and at other community colleges, as they provide justification for the costs and time necessary to put on numerous civic programs and events, as well as support for civic educators who argue that students will be more civically engaged if they are repeatedly exposed to civic opportunities.

Does the Type of Cocurricular Presentation Matter?   The second research question assessed whether the type of cocurricular civic activity affected respondents' self-reported levels of civic engagement and commitment. This analysis focused on differences between the group attending the race and ethnicity Campus Conversations and those who viewed the documentary *A Place at the Table.* (Because only 10 attendees from the Clergy Beyond Borders filled out the survey, it was excluded from this analysis.) For this research question, I conducted a Wilcoxon rank sum to determine if there were measurable and statistically significant differences in the means of the two activity groups. In short, the hunger documentary *A Place at the Table* appeared to be a more powerful civic experience than the Campus Conversations, as measured by survey respondents' ratings of their civic attitudes, civic behaviors, political engagement, and global understanding.

More specifically, among the two types of activities, there were statistically significant differences in the mean responses to six questions, with the hunger documentary being the more powerful cocurricular event in all instances. These questions were: "I will participate in a boycott/buycott to support a social issue"; "My views of voting have not changed"; "My thinking about the issue presented has expanded"; "I intend to explore a serve learning opportunity in the community"; "I will raise money for a charitable organization"; and "I will sign a petition related to the issue presented." Clearly, these results show that attendees at the hunger documentary event exhibited demonstrably higher levels of civic engagement than attendees at the Campus Conversations.

Discussion and Implications

This analysis provides strong support for the provision of multiple cocurricular civic activities on community college campuses. This is particularly relevant as our communities have very real problems—*megachallenges*, as David Mathews (2008) calls them—that can be at least partially addressed by an increase in civic responsibility among our citizens. This is especially true for Allegany County due to the atrophy of legacy industries and the resulting outmigration of the population and diminishing tax base.

The More, the Better. Results from this analysis demonstrate that individuals who attend multiple civic activities exhibit higher levels of civic engagement than those who attend only one event, and that in many areas, the more civic activities a student (or faculty member, or administrator) attends, the better. Attendees at ACM's cocurricular civic presentations—especially those who attended more than one—demonstrated a commitment to solving problems in the community and using petitions as a form of political engagement. It is encouraging to see the foundation of the bridge between the classroom and the community being constructed at ACM. However, further research will be required to determine whether survey respondents actually *did* demonstrate a greater commitment to solving problems in the community; intentions are not the same as actions. Nonetheless, ACM's assumption is that increasing the civic capacity and attitudes of TDC attendees will result in a greater likelihood of civic action.

It is also encouraging to see that the more civic presentations a person attends, the more likely they are to feel a sense of responsibility to use their knowledge to address a global issue. Given our unique geographical location and heritage, many ACM students are unaware of issues outside of our region (which is somewhat ironic, given our proximity to Washington, DC). But many students are the first in their families to attend college, and some have never travelled beyond the tristate area. The results of this analysis appear to indicate that cocurricular civic presentations can serve to introduce students to other ways of thinking and living, in effect helping them to become global citizens. Again, further research is necessary to test whether these self-ratings of global understanding actually result in greater civic engagement; we hope to begin to test this after additional TDC presentations and eventually through time-series analyses.

The Type of Presentation Matters. As noted previously, the hunger documentary was more effective in yielding higher levels of civic engagement than Campus Conversations on the topic of race and ethnicity. One reason for this might be the discussion that followed the screening of *A Place at the Table*, which centered on the need to continue the conversation about hunger in our community and to better coordinate efforts among the various organizations working to address the issue. ACM and its students will not be able to address all of the hunger issues in our community, but we can provide the organizational space to conduct conversations such as this one that can lead to a more efficient use of our limited community resources.

We do not know why the Campus Conversations affected respondents' self-ratings of civic engagement to a lesser degree. All of the conversations used a National Issues Forum format to bring people together to talk about issues of race and ethnicity. In deliberative dialogues, participants are asked to weigh multiple perspectives on race and ethnicity and consider what divides us—and also to build upon what we have in common.

This was the first time that the college held an organized conversation on the subject since the construction of student housing brought a larger African-American population to the college. The topic of race and ethnicity was chosen by our international student club and clearly struck a chord on our campus; in response to an overwhelming demand, we were forced to call extra facilitators into service and to schedule additional sessions. We also asked faculty not to send their entire class to the dialogues and instead made arrangements to facilitate the conversations during regular class meetings.

Once again, the steering committee's goal was not to solve all of the race issues on our campus through deliberative dialogues—an unrealistic expectation—but instead to create an enlarged mentality in our student body concerning race and ethnicity. And indeed, after the dialogues, many students claimed the emergence of new ways of thinking about these issues. They also recognized a need for continued and deepening conversations on this important topic.

So why didn't the dialogues produce the same levels of civic engagement as the hunger documentary? It is possible that the Campus Conversations spurred changes in students' thinking in ways that pertained more specifically to the issue at hand, rather than to broader civic attitudes and behaviors. Furthermore, it may be that attendees at the race and ethnicity dialogues had higher baseline levels of civic engagement than those viewing the hunger documentary or that certain presentation *methods* (documentaries vs. facilitated conversations, for example) may be more effective in influencing attendees' civic engagement. Further research will be required to shed light on whether different presentation formats are more likely than others to influence the civic attitudes and behaviors of students.

The Power of Cocurricular Presentations.   Broadly speaking, results from this study reinforce the idea that cocurricular presentations are an effective way of developing civic engagement on community college campuses. Although a civic engagement *curricular* pathway is ultimately the goal at ACM, as it is necessary for creating an enduring civic culture at the college, cocurricular presentations appear to be a viable way to create a civic foundation on campus.

It must be noted that as it proceeds into its third year, TDC at ACM is still in its infancy. The idea of civic engagement is relatively new to the campus. Although faculty support and buy-in are increasing, many professors are still unsure about how to create civic engagement opportunities for their students. In cocurricular presentations, we have found an effective way to introduce these ideas and begin a conversation with faculty, staff, and administrators about how we might coconstruct a civic culture. The steering committee has also used the TDC work to leverage an AmeriCorps position (and possibly a budgeted staff position next year) to lead the civic engagement work as a curricular pathway is developed. By design, this person will sit on the steering committee and report to the TDC campus coordinator to ensure integration of the curricular and cocurricular pathways. Additionally, the committee has conducted three professional development workshops, as well as additional one-on-one sessions, in order to assist faculty in infusing civic engagement into their curricula. The data are still emerging, but the preliminary results are promising: Last year three faculty members offered service learning or civic engagement opportunities to roughly 35 students. This year 13 professors and over 300 students signed up, and another handful of faculty are in the process of exploring civic options for their courses.

Furthermore, the cocurricular presentations have allowed TDC at ACM to create a greater profile in our larger community; marketing people describe this as "building the brand." All of our events have been covered in the local paper, with many of them garnering prominent coverage in the Local and Slice of Life sections. On occasion, our presentations have also received front page coverage or mention in the Editorial section. Furthermore, local radio stations have promoted the TDC events, airing interviews and public-service announcements. The TDC steering committee has made it clear in all of its marketing and public relations that the events are free and open to the public, hoping to draw greater attendance from the community to continue to build that academic–civic bridge. Even with this effort to draw the community to the presentations, our primary audience still remains the students.

Civic Engagement at Rural Community Colleges.   This ability to use local media outlets to advertise civic events may be an advantage that rural community colleges have in comparison to their urban counterparts. Likewise, the rural area provides a sense of place and is also more likely to define a person's sense of identity. This is especially true in Allegany County as we are located at the foothills of the Appalachian Mountains. Local residents identify themselves by the mountains, and our area is affectionately described as the "mountain-side of Maryland." People tend to know each other and enjoy a network of close relationships. Service learning and civic engagement is facilitated by existing in such a close knit community. Students are more likely to be "insiders" of their community so they can rely upon these networks in order to identify areas of need and to draw upon resources to help meet those needs. Also, in a small rural setting, the results of civic engagement activities are often immediate, visible, and obvious. Students can see the fruits of their civic labor and the impact they have made on their college and in their community.

Finally, small rural colleges tend to have smaller bureaucracies—they are often more accessible and less hierarchal. This means less resistance and fewer structural impediments to civic engagement programs. This also means that the programs can be more nimble and responsive to community needs in an expeditious manner. This is true at ACM, as the only nodes of decision making that need to be addressed external to the steering committee exist at the level of the president and the vice president of academic affairs. Both individuals have been unwavering supporters of The

Democracy Commitment from the start, and with their support there have been few bureaucratic impediments to our work.

Conclusion

In 3 short years, the civic engagement work of TDC at ACM has grown. The unique qualities of the initiative that were present at the beginning are still present today. However, these qualities, which were initially viewed as concerns—being a small, rural college, using cocurricular presentations instead of infusing civic work directly into the curriculum, being guided by a steering committee of dedicated faculty and staff—have been recognized and embraced as unique strengths. Our hope is that by sharing the results of this study, other colleges with the same "constraints" will be emboldened to create civic programs that work within their unique circumstances to benefit their students, campuses, and communities.

References

Eddy, P. (2007). Grocery store politics: Leading the rural community college. *Community College Journal of Research and Practice, 31*(4), 271–290.

Emory, M., & Flora, C. (2006). Spiraling-up: Mapping community transformation with community capitals framework. *Journal of the Community Development Society, 37*(1), 19–35.

Finlay, A. (2011). Civic learning and democratic engagements: A review of the literature on civic engagement in postsecondary education. Retrieved from https://www.aacu .org/sites/default/files/files/CLDE/LiteratureReview.pdf.

Gallini, S., & Moely, B. (2003). Service-learning and engagement, academic challenge, and retention. *Michigan Journal of Community Service Learning, 10*(1), 5–14.

Holton, N. (2009). Rural service learning: Turning special challenges into great opportunities. Journal for Civic Commitment. Retrieved from http://ccncce.org/articles/rural-service-learning-turning-special-challenges-into-great-opportunities/.

Hoy, A., & Meisel, W. (2008). *Civic engagement at the center: Building democracy through integrated co-curricular and curricular experience.* Washington, DC: American Association of Colleges and Universities.

Keen, C., & Hall, K. (2009). Engaging with difference matters: Longitudinal student outcomes of co-curricular service-learning programs. *Journal of Higher Education, 80*(1), 59–79.

Stoecker, R., & Schmidt, C. (2008, August). *Geographic disparities in access to service learning.* Paper presented at the 2008 annual meeting of the Rural Sociological Society, Manchester, NH. Retrieved from http://comm-org.wisc.edu/drafts/wisl.htm.

Vogelsang, L. J., & Astin, A. W. (2005). *Post-college civic engagement among graduates* (HERI Research Report no. 2). Los Angeles: Higher Education Research Institute.

Kurt Hoffman is interim senior vice president of instructional and student affairs and TDC coordinator at Allegany College of Maryland.

New Directions for Community Colleges • DOI: 10.1002/cc

11

This chapter describes the individual and institutional factors leading to greater civic outcomes among students at four The Democracy Commitment (TDC) colleges in California.

The Civic Outcomes of Community College

Carrie B. Kisker, Mallory Angeli Newell, Dayna S. Weintraub

Many community college scholars and leaders believe strongly that community colleges "are uniquely suited to civic engagement and the work of democracy" (Kisker & Ronan, 2012, p. 2). Nonetheless, a chasm remains between educators' beliefs and our current ability to measure the civic capacities of our students. Indeed, few studies have attempted to assess levels of civic engagement among community college students. In 2006, Lopez and Brown found that these students were more likely than high school graduates—but less likely than 4-year college students—to vote or obtain news on a daily basis. They were about as likely as 4-year college students to register to vote or volunteer. Newell (2014) similarly concluded that community college students were somewhat more civically engaged than high school graduates but less engaged than their counterparts at 4-year colleges and universities.

These comparative studies provide some sense of the civic landscape among institutions of higher education but provide little information about the effects of various community college programs and practices aimed at developing students' civic capacities. Prompted by the Lumina Foundation's Degree Qualifications Profile (which lists civic learning as one of the five categories of learning required in associate, bachelor's, and master's degree programs), the American Association of State Colleges and Universities and the Association of American Colleges and Universities recently collaborated on an effort to collect instruments being used by colleges and universities to assess civic learning. The inventory they collected (Reason & Hemer, 2014) reinforces the dearth of instrumentation in this area.

NEW DIRECTIONS FOR COMMUNITY COLLEGES, no. 173, Spring 2016 © 2016 Wiley Periodicals, Inc.
Published online in Wiley Online Library (wileyonlinelibrary.com) • DOI: 10.1002/cc.20195

In an effort to bridge this gap, The Democracy Commitment (TDC)—a national initiative providing a platform for the development and expansion of civic engagement in community colleges—engaged in a pilot examination of the individual and institutional factors leading to greater civic agency, behavior, and knowledge among students at four community colleges in California. This chapter describes the conceptual framework, methods, and results of the California pilot, administered in spring 2014.

Conceptual Framework

Astin's (1993) Input-Environment-Outcome (I-E-O) Model of college impact provides the conceptual frame for this study. The I-E-O model takes into account student characteristics at the time of initial entry to the institution, the environment and experiences to which students are exposed, and finally, students' characteristics or outcomes after exposure to that environment. Our investigation thus presumes that students arrive at community colleges with individual background characteristics—both demographic and behavioral—that provide a baseline for their civic development and that within the community college environment there are multiple programs, practices, policies, people, cultures, and experiences that affect students' civic outcomes.

Methods

In order to collect data on both demographic (input) and college-level (environmental) factors that might influence students' civic outcomes, we developed and administered two instruments in late spring 2014. The first was a civic outcomes survey consisting of 20 multipart questions assessing students' civic agency, behavior, and knowledge after at least 1 year of community college attendance, as well as questions relating to student demographics and enrollment patterns. The second instrument—a questionnaire filled out by a coordinator at each participating institution—asked about college-level factors known to influence student engagement, as well as the various ways in which institutions work to develop civic learning and democratic engagement among their students. Individual questions included in both instruments were informed by a wide swath of cross-disciplinary literature and are discussed in detail in Kisker, Newell, and Ronan (2014, April).

The civic outcomes survey was sent to 34,587 students at three community colleges (one very large, one large, and one medium-sized institution, according to the Carnegie Classifications) and one large community college district in California—all members of The Democracy Commitment. At three of the institutions, the survey was sent to the entire student body, but in the district, the survey was limited to students participating in the Honors College. At three of the institutions the survey was administered online, and at the fourth both online and paper versions were used. A total of 1,756 usable surveys were returned, for an aggregate 5% response rate (response rates varied from 2% to 10% among the four participating institutions). Although we were not able to check for nonresponse bias, a comparison of our results to previously reported voting patterns among community college students indicated that students in our sample voted at rates similar to the national average (Center for Information and Research on Civic Learning and Engagement, 2012). As well, although our aggregate sample included more women than men, more full-timers than part-timers, more Whites than students of color, and fewer students between the ages of 20 and 24 than those in other age groups, the composition of the sample was similar to those from previous survey implementations at one of the four participating colleges (see Kisker, Newell, & Ronan, 2014, April).

Data analysis occurred in three stages. First, we performed descriptive and demographic cross-tab analyses of the survey data in order to capture a preliminary snapshot of students' levels of civic agency, behavior, and knowledge. We then conducted a factor analysis, identifying seven factors that explain most of the variance observed in questions related to students' civic outcomes. The seven dependent variables in our analysis are:

- *Civic Leadership Behavior* (joining organizations; holding leadership roles; service learning; and raising money for a campaign, party, or group)
- *Political Behavior* (working on a campaign; attending a march, rally, protest, or boycott; raising awareness about an issue, campaign, or group; persuading others to vote for a particular candidate or party; and contacting public officials or the media)
- *Electoral Participation* (signing a petition, registering to vote, and voting)
- *Civic Agency* (view of self as part of campus or larger community, as someone who values helping others, as someone with a voice, and as someone with something to offer the world; belief that after college they will promote social change, become a leader, help others, and be an integral part of society)
- *Civic Capacity* (increased ability to converse with and understand others, have views challenged, and voice concerns; belief in ability to seek information to develop an informed view on an issue, communicate with someone whose views are different, and effect change in society)
- *Increased Civic Knowledge* (self-reported gains in knowledge of global, national, and community issues)
- *Correct Answers to Civic Knowledge Questions* (three questions dealing with national, state, and local political understanding)

In addition to the seven dependent variables, we also used factor analysis to create three pretest variables (civic leadership behavior, political behavior, and electoral participation prior to entering college) as well as four composite measures comprising related questions from the institutional questionnaire (institutional intentionality around civic engagement, academic focus on civic engagement, cocurricular focus on civic engagement, and civic engagement in faculty professional development and tenure/advancement policies).

Finally, we ran regressions on each of the seven dependent variables in order to identify the individual and institutional factors associated with greater civic outcomes. Each regression used a stepwise technique, allowing students' precollege behaviors to enter the model first, followed by student characteristics, college characteristics, and finally, student behaviors while in college. This process holds constant all of the variables that have already entered the model, allowing us to assess how much each additional variable contributes to the percentage of variance that can be explained by the analysis (Astin, 2002).

Descriptive Results of the Civic Outcomes Survey

Descriptive results of the civic outcomes survey show that community college students are reasonably engaged in civic or political activities, although the percentage of students engaged in a given activity is inversely related to the amount of time or energy that activity requires. For example, nearly half of all respondents indicated that since entering college they have discussed politics regularly (51%) or voted in a federal, state, or local election (47%), but only 24% had contacted public officials or the media and just 16% reported attending a march, rally, boycott, or protest.

Full-time and part-time students demonstrated similar rates of civic behavior but in different activities. For example, full-timers were more likely to join a group or organization and volunteer in the community, whereas part-timers were more likely to vote or contact public officials or the media. Similarly, female and male students engaged at about the same rate but in different activities. Female students were more likely to work without pay in the community; raise money for a campaign, party, or group; and raise awareness about an issue, campaign, party or group. Male students were more likely to obtain news regularly, persuade others to vote for a particular candidate or party, and vote. These results mirror those of Jenkins (2005), Marcelo, Lopez, and Kirby (2007), and Verba, Schlozman, and Brady (1995), which show that women are more likely to be engaged in community-based activities, whereas men are often more engaged in political activities.

Predictive Results of the Civic Outcomes Survey

Although we are most concerned with the institutional variables leading to civic outcomes—in other words, those characteristics and behaviors over which community colleges have at least some control—it is worth mentioning a few individual predictors of civic outcomes.

NEW DIRECTIONS FOR COMMUNITY COLLEGES • DOI: 10.1002/cc

Individual Predictors of Community College Civic Outcomes.   Controlling for students' precollege behaviors, our analyses showed that Latino heritage positively contributes to Electoral Participation and Civic Agency and that females are more likely than males to demonstrate higher levels of Civic Capacity. Also, speaking English at home is positively associated with Electoral Participation but negatively related to Civic Capacity and Increased Civic Knowledge (perhaps because native English speakers enter college with a higher level of civic understanding than those from immigrant families). Furthermore, age is associated with higher levels of Political Behavior and Civic Agency; full-time enrollment contributes to higher levels of Civic Capacity, Civic Agency, and Increased Civic Knowledge; and the more credits students earn at a community college the more likely they are to demonstrate most civic outcomes. Furthermore, higher parental income, speaking English at home, and age are positively associated with Correctly Answering Civic Questions, whereas females, Asians, Latinos, and those who identify as Other Race/Ethnicity were less likely to answer the questions correctly.

Institutional Predictors of Community College Civic Outcomes.   In order to determine how much influence community colleges have on students' civic outcomes, we compared the intermediate R^2 values (the percentage of variance in each dependent variable accounted for by students' precollege behaviors and demographics) with the R^2 after all variables were taken into account. After the precollege variables entered the models, intermediate R^2 values ranged from .06 to .33. After the environmental variables (college characteristics and college student behaviors) entered, final R^2 values ranged from .16 to .68, with those dependent variables that are easier to quantify (specifically, the behavioral factors and correctly answering civic questions) falling on the higher end of the range. What is clear from this comparison is that community colleges have a substantial ability to influence students' civic outcomes. Indeed, college characteristics and college student behaviors account for the majority of the total R^2 for Civic Leadership (66%), Correctly Answer Civic Questions (70%), Civic Agency (50%), Civic Capacity (61%), and Increased Civic Knowledge (63%). Furthermore, environmental factors explain between 24% and 34%, respectively, of students' Electoral Participation and Political Behavior, even though this type of involvement in democratic processes may be only loosely tied to students' educational goals and experiences.

In addition to examining the total amount of variance that can be explained by environmental variables, we also identified the specific college characteristics and college student behaviors that lead to greater civic outcomes. Our analysis showed that community colleges with above-average percentages of full-time faculty are associated with higher levels of Civic Agency and Increased Civic Knowledge. Students from colleges that incorporate civic engagement into their professional development programs or their faculty tenure/advancement procedures are also more likely to demonstrate Civic Agency and Increased Civic Knowledge. Finally, institutional intentionality toward civic engagement (civic engagement mentioned in mission or strategic plan and/or a dedicated center for student engagement on campus) is associated with Increased Civic Knowledge and more students Correctly Answering Civic Questions. Despite the fact that results related to college characteristics must be interpreted with some degree of caution due to the small number of institutions in this pilot study, these findings indicate that by making visible and meaningful institutional commitments to civic learning and democratic engagement, community colleges can do much to improve their students' civic outcomes.

Although collegewide support for civic engagement may be important, it is clear from our analysis that specific student behaviors while in college may be the strongest predictors of civic outcomes. Indeed, obtaining news regularly, discussing politics regularly, volunteering in the community, and voting in student elections are each positively associated with at least six of the seven dependent variables. Discussing politics, volunteering, and voting in student elections show particularly strong associations with the dependent variables, indicating that the more community colleges work to encourage these behaviors, the more likely it is that their students will display the civic agency, capacities, behaviors, and knowledge necessary to participate meaningfully in a democratic society.

What Can We Take Away from This Analysis (and Where Do We Go from Here)?

The results of this pilot study provide preliminary yet meaningful information about community college students' civic outcomes, both in terms of the frequency and ways in which students engage in civic or political activities, as well the substantial amount of influence community colleges appear to have over students' civic agency, behavior, and knowledge. These results add much to the nascent scholarly literature on community college civic outcomes, but perhaps most important, they provide support for the myriad ways community colleges across the country—especially those associated with The Democracy Commitment—are working to encourage civic and democratic engagement on their campuses.

However, as with most pilot studies, there are several inherent limitations, including a low response rate, a lack of standardization in the way the survey was implemented at the four institutions, and an overrepresentation of certain groups among respondents. Furthermore, the results—especially those related to college characteristics—must be interpreted with some caution due to the small number of participating institutions. Finally, although we found that college student behaviors are powerfully associated with civic outcomes—a finding that provides community colleges with much practical information about how they might work to improve civic outcomes—there exists a chicken-and-egg problem in interpreting the results. For example, does regularly discussing politics lead to greater civic agency? Or does increased civic agency cause students to engage in more political discussions? A plausible argument can be made that students' behaviors lead to changes in the way they view themselves and their capacity to communicate with others and effect change (after all, this assumption underlies many tenets of teaching and learning, not to mention the field of behavioral psychology), but we cannot know this for sure.

Many of the limitations present in this study will be addressed in the next stage of our work, which includes an examination of civic outcomes at 10–15 community colleges across the country in spring 2015. Institutions participating in this national pilot will follow a standardized procedure for administering the survey and will check for nonresponse bias. Furthermore, the greater diversity of institutions (geographically and in terms of size, student demographics, and civic programs and practices) will allow for much more variation in both student and college characteristics. We have also modified both the civic outcomes survey and institutional questionnaire in preparation for the 2015 national pilot. Specifically, we added scaled responses to many previously dichotomous (yes/no) questions, which should allow for a more nuanced analysis of the individual and institutional factors leading to community college civic outcomes.

Despite its limitations, the results of the California pilot indicate that community colleges can and do play an important role in shaping students' civic lives. By making visible and measurable commitments to civic learning and democratic engagement on campus, and by creating opportunities for students to interact with one another, wrestle with thorny social or political issues, and engage in their communities, colleges can help create informed citizens who are skilled in democratic practices and committed to lifelong engagement.

References

Astin, A. W. (1993). *What matters in college? Four critical years revisited.* San Francisco: Jossey-Bass.

Astin, A. W. (2002). *Assessment for excellence: The philosophy and practice of assessment and evaluation in higher education.* Westport, CT: American Council on Education and Oryx Press.

Center for Information and Research on Civic Learning and Engagement. (2012). *National study of learning, voting, and engagement: Comparison groups.* Medford, MA: Tufts University, Jonathan M. Tisch College of Citizenship and Public Service.

Jenkins, K. (2005). *Gender and civic engagement: Secondary analysis of survey data.* College Park, MD: Center for Information and Research on Civic Learning and Engagement.

Kisker, C. B., & Ronan, B. (2012). *Civic engagement in community colleges: Mission, institutionalization, and future prospects.* Dayton, OH: Kettering Foundation.

Kisker, C. B., Newell, M. A., & Ronan, B. (2014, April). Assessing students' civic agency, behavior, and knowledge at 4 TDC colleges. Paper presented at the 56th annual Council for the Study of Community Colleges conference, Washington, DC.

Lopez, M. H., & Brown, B. (2006). *Civic engagement among 2-year and 4-year college students*. Medford, MA: Center for Information and Research on Civic Learning and Engagement.

Marcelo, K. B., Lopez, M. H., & Kirby, E. H. (2007).*Civic engagement among young men and women*. Washington, DC: Center for Information and Research on Civic Learning and Engagement.

Newell, M. A. (2014). America's democracy colleges: The civic engagement of community college students. *Community College Journal of Research and Practice, 38*(9), 794–810.

Reason, R., & Hemer, K. (2014). *Civic learning and engagement: A review of the literature on civic learning, assessment, and instruments*. Ames, IA: Iowa State University, Research Institute for Studies in Education.

Verba, S., Schlozman, K. L., & Brady, H. E. (1995). *Voice and equality: Civic voluntarism in American politics*. New York: Harper & Row.

CARRIE B. KISKER *is an education research and policy consultant in Los Angeles, California, and a director of the Center for the Study of Community Colleges.*

MALLORY ANGELI NEWELL *is director of research and planning at De Anza College.*

DAYNA S. WEINTRAUB *is a doctoral candidate at UCLA's Graduate School of Education and Information Sciences.*

12

This chapter describes Skyline College's student-centered approach to campus dialogue and deliberation and assesses the transferability of these skills to civic, workplace, and personal settings.

Empowering and Transforming a Community of Learners via a Student-Centered Approach to Campus Dialogue and Deliberation

Jennifer Mair

There is something imperative in the work of student and community engagement for me—partially a sense of ethical and social responsibility and partially self-interested survival. When we look at the sheer number and potential impact of important issues looming over society without clear resolution—unsustainable consumption, energy needs and costs to the environment, water shortages and pollution, nuclear proliferation in unstable political environments and regimes—it prompts some of us to ask "What can we do?" Just as important as *what* we do is *how* we do it. Civic engagement activities and methods aim for broad, direct participation in democratic processes, inviting and prompting students and citizens to participate in addressing the problems and issues that directly affect them. This kind of civic engagement goes deeper than community service and service learning that are typically focused on addressing symptoms of social problems. It is achieved by "bringing broad groups of citizens together to develop shared understanding, build capacity, and systemically address the problems themselves" (Carcasson, 2013, p. 19).

I believe the current low levels of public participation in our democracy are not primarily due to a lack of interest and desire to participate in public life. Rather, civic disinterest stems from a perceived lack of opportunity for meaningful participation and a sense that we don't have a real impact on the decision making and outcomes that benefit the common good. The civic

New Directions for Community Colleges, no. 173, Spring 2016 © 2016 Wiley Periodicals, Inc.
Published online in Wiley Online Library (wileyonlinelibrary.com) • DOI: 10.1002/cc.20196

actions of voting, contacting a representative, speaking at public meetings, and even volunteering are limited ways for citizens to participate, seeming to have no real impact on the decisions or issues that directly affect our communities.

Yet when opportunities are created for citizens to be heard and engaged in decisions that affect them, many more engage in the political process. Meaningful participation includes dialogue that allows for telling our stories and perspectives, revealing underlying values and assumptions, hearing diverse viewpoints, and deliberating options and alternatives to address public concerns and issues. It also means that the outcomes of public participation matter to the ultimate outcomes and decisions made by those in positions of power. Rather than relying solely on expert or adversarial approaches to public debate and problem solving, dialogue and deliberative engagement "rely on citizens, not just experts or politicians, to be deeply involved in public decision making. Ideally, citizens come together and consider relevant facts and values from multiple perspectives, listen to one another in order to think critically about the various options ... and ultimately come to some conclusion for various forms of action in the form of a reasoned public judgment" (Carcasson, 2013, pp. 12–13).

This requires a fundamental change in the patterns of participation and communication that make up modern politics and decision making. We need to create pathways and opportunities for meaningful public participation. By engaging broad groups of students and citizens, our public conversations can lead to enhanced capacity to act together to solve our social problems. This change is needed on multiple levels, and educational institutions—community colleges in particular—are critical arenas for social and political change. Educational institutions are embedded in the fabric of our communities, and are well positioned to address what Carcasson (2013) sees as "the primary problem with deliberative engagement ... how to build support for it, and ultimately make it a habit in our communities" (p. 14).

As a communication instructor at Skyline College in California, and a founder of Skyline's Center for Community Engagement, I am keenly aware that transforming our patterns of communication to rely on informed dialogue and deliberation, rather than debate and argument, is crucial to transforming our personal and political spheres—our relationships and our communities. Teaching and modeling dialogue and deliberation skills to students and citizens—and creating opportunities to use these skills in relation to issues that matter—begins to transform patterns of unproductive debate and apathy, providing foundational skills and processes for effective civic participation. Dialogue and deliberation skills are critical to the success of public participation processes that depend on civility and the willingness to listen to each other, think together, and act together.

Dialogue and deliberation skills have a place in every sphere of life. They support productive communication and navigation of challenging conversations and situations in all of our relationships, whether in the workplace, in our homes, or in our communities. The skills central to public dialogue and deliberation, identified as essential outcomes of both a college education and democratic practice, include listening deeply to other points of view, exploring new ideas and perspectives, searching for points of agreement, and bringing unexamined assumptions into the open. Dialogue and deliberation skills need to be modeled and practiced to be incorporated meaningfully into our conflict management and decision-making processes. And as Ronan (2011) points out, learning this level of civic literacy and citizenship takes time: "Students must develop the knowledge and skills to truly act as citizens" (p. 1). Yet teaching our students to effectively communicate with, listen to, and collaborate with others is essential for our campuses, our democracy, and our workplaces. Hart Research Associates (2013) recently surveyed employers, asking about the priorities and skills sets they seek when hiring new workers. The results of this survey highlight the importance of dialogue and deliberation skills to a thriving workplace: Nearly all those surveyed agree that a candidate's demonstrated capacity to think critically, communicate clearly, and solve complex problems is more important than their undergraduate major. More than three in four employers say they want colleges to place more emphasis on helping students develop five key learning outcomes: critical thinking, complex problem solving, written and oral communication, and applied knowledge in real-world settings.

Real-world settings contain what are known as wicked problems, and "addressing wicked problems demands effective collaboration and communication across multiple perspectives" (Carcasson, 2013, p. 5). This is the focus of my work at Skyline College.

Dialogue and Deliberation at Skyline College

At Skyline College, teaching dialogue and deliberation skills and creating opportunities for students to meaningfully use these skills occur in four primary ways. The first is through workshops teaching dialogue, deliberation, and facilitation skills. These workshops teach students the fundamental principles and skills of dialogue and dialogue facilitation, as well as how dialogue is a different form of communication than argument and debate. Students learn to deeply listen and understand what others are thinking, invite diverse voices and perspectives into the conversation, and apply dialogue and facilitation skills in sensitive and contentious situations. The workshops provide opportunities to practice these skills in a safe environment, allowing students to reflect together on what they are learning.

The second method of engaging students involves organizing and convening campus forums. Students trained in the dialogue and facilitation workshops serve as facilitators and recorders of the conversations. Campus forums are designed to begin with exploratory dialogues that move into deliberative processes, focusing on topics such as diversity appreciation, building unity across difference, interfaith dialogues, student success and engagement, campus sustainability, and improving our campus and community. We use different designs for different forums depending upon the topics and desired outcomes, but successful process designs include the National Issues Forums, World Café, the Public Conversations Project, the Public Dialogue Consortium, and others. In each of these forums, students participate in small, student-facilitated group dialogues with an agreed-upon set of ground rules. They are designed to begin with time for students to share their stories and experiences on a particular topic, then participants move into thinking together, sharing their best ideas for addressing specific issues. They culminate in deliberative processes, which include group selection of the best ideas and actions to be taken, often incorporating the use of keypad voting to assist in collective decision making and the surfacing of collective wisdom.

The third track of my work at Skyline College includes inspiring and supporting students to take collective action. Through our President's Innovation Fund, I run a grant program called Skyline Students Step Up. Student-led groups are encouraged and supported to "step up" and initiate project ideas to improve our campus and community. Campus forums are organized to both kick off and generate ideas for these projects and later to have Skyline students deliberate and vote for the groups who will receive funding to see their projects through. Student-led projects that have been implemented as a result of these grants have included conducting an analysis of waste diversion to encourage our campus and city to compost, improving the veterans' center, supporting undocumented students, installing hydration stations on campus to help limit the use of disposable plastic water bottles, encouraging carpooling and ridesharing, hosting a regular open mic night, and planting and maintaining a community garden.

Finally, Skyline offers a credit-based internship program that—through a semester-long independent study course—trains and involves students in the work of dialogue, deliberation, and community engagement, as well as in the important and time-consuming work of community outreach, from face-to-face interviews to social media messaging. Through this internship program, students gain valuable, practical experience and confidence in their roles as dialogue facilitators and learn the principles of public engagement, event design, and community coordination.

I'll readily admit to incentivizing students to participate in these four activities—food and extra credit are obvious ways to entice students into a room and expose them to public engagement processes. They are often pleasantly surprised that they enjoyed and learned much from the events and workshops. They also report appreciating being able to meet new people, express their voices and perspectives, learn about others' beliefs, and gain a stronger sense of community.

Although some outcomes or results of these four tracks of student engagement are concrete and immediate (i.e., student project accomplishments and good feelings about what they have learned), the real impetus for the work is the desire to empower students to see that their individual and collective actions make a difference. Providing opportunities to give students a voice, engaging them in issues that affect them, and teaching and modeling the participatory processes and communication skills necessary to successfully navigate dialogue and deliberation give me hope that students will take these skills and processes into other spheres of their lives.

Investigating the Transferability of Dialogue and Deliberation Skills

Although experience and instinct have led me to believe that student-centered trainings and events focused on dialogue and deliberation ultimately lead to more effective communication skills and processes in both civic and personal spheres, there has been little empirical evidence related to the specific outcomes of this work or students' ability to transfer skills from one milieu to another. Thus, I developed an open-ended questionnaire to investigate if and how Skyline students (and former students) are able to transfer their dialogue and deliberation skills to the workplace, their families, and other settings. In fall 2013, I administered the questionnaire via e-mail to 110 students who had participated in dialogue and facilitation skills workshops between spring 2011 and spring 2013. I also administered the questionnaire in person to 51 students who participated in a fall 2013 workshop and another 60 students who participated in a campus forum the same semester, many of whom had previously completed the workshop training. Students were asked to self-report on their comfort level applying dialogue and deliberation skills in specific contexts. They were also asked to evaluate which skills have been most relevant or useful to them in specific, challenging situations and conversations. Questions were devised according to the three factors of *relevancy*, *responsibility*, and *reality* (Claxton, 2007).

Twenty-seven of the 110 students who completed a dialogue and facilitation skills training workshop between spring 2011 and spring 2013 completed the questionnaire (a response rate of 25%), as did all of the 51 students who completed a similar workshop in fall 2013. An additional 42 campus forum participants completed the survey (a response rate of 70%).

Analyses of questionnaire results clearly indicate that dialogue and deliberation skills are perceived as immediately valuable to student participants. Students are able to transfer the dialogue and deliberation skills they learn to other contexts, from the public spheres of work and community to the personal spheres of friends, family, and significant others. Further, it is apparent that students feel significantly more prepared, inspired, and responsible for addressing social issues with others as a result of their participation in a workshop and/or forum. For example, 98% of diversity forum participants reported that they *felt more responsibility to open up a dialogue with others when encountering prejudice, discrimination, and stereotyping to create mutual understanding and respect*. Similarly, 78% of sustainability forum participants stated that they *are more inspired to be involved in important issues for their campus and community*. This sense of agency and desire to engage with others in meaningful ways is reinforced by students' open-ended responses to survey questions. Indeed, these responses made clear that nearly all questionnaire respondents were more comfortable with both the idea of dialogue and deliberation and the skills essential to the processes. For example, one student wrote: "I learned to interact with people in a way I never did before. I learned the value of people's opinions and how everyone's view is different." Another claimed, "What I learned through the deliberations was different opinions and views we may have not thought of before, which goes to prove that collective wisdom is much greater than individual wisdom. With hearing many different people's thoughts on the topic you go further into depth on the wicked issue each time you choose to talk about it."

Furthermore, nearly 9 out of 10 students strongly agreed or agreed that they were more willing to participate in conversations that are difficult in order to problem solve and come to a mutual understanding. As one wrote, "Being able to understand what the other person is saying and accepting their opinions regardless of whether I agree or not are important skills. It helped me avoid fights where I would insist that my viewpoint is right." Another added, "I learned to ask questions to deepen my understanding of another person's standpoint in order to get to the truth or main point rather than moving in misunderstanding and reactions."

Students were also asked to specify with whom and in what contexts they have applied their dialogue and facilitation skills. The vast majority agreed they have used or will use their skills during important and difficult conversations with community members and with coworkers or classmates. Students' open-ended responses about how and where they have applied their dialogue and deliberation skills were especially encouraging and make clear that students are applying and intending to apply these skills in public contexts to enhance work relationships and experiences. As one former student wrote, "I have actually had the opportunity to utilize all skills learned in the workshop on a daily basis. I am a manager/leader of a team of 35 people and I often have to facilitate team meetings, and one-on-one meetings with team members, and I utilize most skills I learned for client resolution issues that I come across. In my new field as paralegal, the skills that I have acquired have helped mediate client communication with their attorney."

Another student planned to apply her skills in a more civic arena: "I am now 10 times more interested in volunteering when there are events in my community. Before this experience, I was always aware of this issue in the community but I never felt that people were concerned enough to participate. Therefore it discouraged me to do things for my community. But after engaging the community and conducting interviews on this topic, I can see that people do care. It definitely opened my eyes to the many perspectives in the world regarding this issue. It makes me want to change myself so I can influence other people to change their lifestyles."

Nearly all questionnaire respondents also indicated a willingness to use their new skills *in important and difficult conversations with family, friends, or significant others.* The following statements typified student responses:

- "I learned how to facilitate effective communication methods to resolve conflicts. I will implement these skills at home within the family structure."
- "Acknowledging what the other person has said and using dual perspective has been the skills I used the most with my significant other because it helped me understand him more and to connect with him better."
- "I have actively listened to my godmother when she is giving me her perspective of things, although I do not agree I listen and try to understand her perspective."

Discussion

It is evident that the dialogue and deliberation skills students learn and practice during Skyline's workshops and forums are being successfully transferred to other areas of their lives, making real and positive impacts in both the public and private spheres. This is the case for both recent workshop participants and those who had engaged between 6 and 18 months before. This indicates that students' dialogue and deliberation skills were still being put to use in various and productive ways even after students left the institution.

Indeed, those students who had time to practice their skills in campus forums or other settings were most confident in their ability to use them in civic, workplace, or personal settings. I believe this is due partially to students being unsure of how their skills will hold up in *real-world* situations as opposed to somewhat tough but theoretical role-play scenarios. Providing real-life experiences and opportunities to practice these skills reinforces students' learning and helps them gain the additional confidence they need to apply them outside the college environment.

Lessons Learned

Although at times the work of student and civic engagement feels time-consuming and incremental and it can be challenging to assess hard outcomes, the rewards are intrinsic and reinforced by student feedback. I have students who return months and years later to report a triumphant circumstance where they were able to use their skills to successfully navigate or facilitate a difficult conversation or situation. After years of doing this work at Skyline College, I have seen the administration, faculty, staff, and student leaders initiate and plan for participatory processes (both with and without my input) in division meetings, campus and community summits, and classrooms. There is a growing awareness of the value of planning for participatory public processes and inviting public input in decision making to support the desire for collective action. It has been incredibly rewarding to see inspired students taking action to improve Skyline College and the communities within and around it.

However, implementing dialogue and deliberation training is not a simple task. One of the challenges I have encountered is connecting the outcomes of these deliberative processes to meaningful outcomes for the campus (and therefore more meaningful outcomes for participants). I have become more adept at this over the years and continue to seek out connections with other campus groups and organizations that produce synergy. A successful example of this is working toward increased campus sustainability by collaborating with college and district sustainability programs and initiatives. Also, we continue to organize campus forums that invite student participation into decision-making and leadership roles.

Another significant challenge on our campus is to continue finding ways to incorporate participatory experiences, dialogue, and deliberation into completion and transfer pathways. Too often we are asking students who are already overwhelmed to give more. Although they are inspired to participate, they are often weary of all they need to manage in terms of courses, work, and families. Creating opportunities for course credit, internships, and certificate programs is important to meaningfully integrate the work of dialogue, deliberation, and student engagement into our institution as well as into the lives of our students.

It is evident that not everyone has the same working knowledge of what is meant by civic or student engagement, nor the communication skills and principles essential to dialogue and deliberation. I often encounter blank looks when I describe the work that I do, or receive varying opinions about how to "get things done" or "produce outcomes." Efficient, concrete outcomes are always desirable, yet they are secondary to students' learning and applying skills. Although at times I have felt the lone soldier promoting this work on our campus, the recognition the work has garnered has provided the foundation for a successful collaborative of supportive faculty, staff, and students, many of whom are now involved in the newly founded Skyline College Center for Community Engagement.

The work of developing the skills and knowledge critical to civic literacy and citizenship takes time—both our students and our institutions need to first learn and then practice these skills in meaningful ways. However, the vision of an informed citizenry acting purposefully, collaboratively, and consistently to address critical issues or *wicked problems* makes it worth the investment.

NEW DIRECTIONS FOR COMMUNITY COLLEGES • DOI: 10.1002/cc

References

Carcasson, M. (2013). *Rethinking civic engagement on campus: The overarching potential of deliberative practice.* Dayton, OH: Kettering Foundation.

Claxton, G. (2007). Expanding young people's capacity to learn. *British Journal of Educational Studies, 55*(2), 1–20.

Hart Research Associates. (2013). *It takes more than a major: Employer priorities for college learning and student success.* Washington, DC: Association of American Colleges and Universities.

Ronan, B. (2011). *The civic spectrum: How students become engaged citizens.* Dayton, OH: Kettering Foundation.

JENNIFER MAIR is a professor of communications at Skyline College.

13

This chapter explores ways that the civic and workforce missions of community colleges might be better integrated in practice, using Minneapolis Community and Technical College as an example.

Bridging the Workforce and Civic Missions of Community Colleges

Lena Jones

Since 2002, I have been a political science faculty member at Minneapolis Community and Technical College (MCTC). Like many community and technical colleges, MCTC has civic and workforce goals that seamlessly coexist within its vision and mission statements. For example, the college's vision is "to be an institution that transforms the community by educating students who are globally aware, *engaged citizens, skillful at their work* and lifelong learners." Its mission is to "make individual dreams achievable by providing access to learning opportunities that prepare students to *live and work in a democratic society* within a global community" through a variety of vehicles, including liberal education, technical education, and workforce development.

However, at MCTC—as at many other colleges—the two goals are often thought of and pursued separately. This reality raised two questions for me: How are the civic and workforce goals viewed by students and employees of the college? And, what are the possibilities and challenges of integrating the civic and workforce missions in practice?

To investigate these questions, our research team (consisting of myself and service learning work–study student Felicia Hamilton) organized several focus groups and facilitated discussions with students, staff, and faculty at MCTC to seek their perspectives about how the civic and workforce missions manifest in the lives of students and employees at the college. This chapter describes what emerged in focus groups with students, as well as several questions raised in facilitated discussions with faculty and staff. The chapter concludes with a reflection on the challenges and possibilities of integrating the civic and workforce missions of community colleges, both at MCTC and elsewhere.

New Directions for Community Colleges, no. 173, Spring 2016 © 2016 Wiley Periodicals, Inc.
Published online in Wiley Online Library (wileyonlinelibrary.com) • DOI: 10.1002/cc.20197

Student Views of MCTC's Civic and Workforce Missions

Although MCTC has vision and mission statements that clearly emphasize its civic and workforce missions, we wanted to investigate whether students connected the two missions in their minds. Therefore, we recruited 24 students to participate in five focus groups conducted in fall 2013 and spring 2014. Twelve of those students were in career and technical education (CTE) programs and the other 12 were in various liberal arts programs. In the focus groups, students were presented with the college's mission and vision statements and asked the following questions:

1. Drawing from your own experiences both inside and outside the classroom, in what ways do you see the college fulfilling its vision to create "engaged citizens" and its mission to prepare students to "live ... in a democratic society"?
2. Drawing from your own experiences both inside and outside the classroom, in what ways do you see the college fulfilling its mission to educate students who are "skillful at their work ... " and prepare students to "work in a democratic society"?

We also asked additional questions about the types of activities and opportunities that students would like to see (both inside and outside of the classroom) related to the college's civic and workforce missions. All focus groups were audio recorded and transcribed verbatim.

Student Views on the Civic Mission of the College. Focus group participants shared a variety of examples of how the college fulfills its civic mission. The responses tended to fall into three categories: (a) out-of-classroom experiences with community organizations, (b) exposure to new ideas and communal learning experiences, and (c) challenging learning environments.

Several students cited experiences connected to courses that either required or encouraged students to work with a community organization through semester-long service learning projects or via shorter-term volunteering activities. Field trips to governmental institutions such as the state capitol and to community organizations were also cited by focus group participants as significant learning experiences that exemplify the college's civic mission. These experiences were also meaningful to students. As one explained, "Going to the Capitol brought to life what happens in cabinet offices."

Students also connected classroom experiences in which they were exposed to new ideas or required to work in groups to the civic mission of the college. They shared experiences where they participated in discussions related to current issues, were exposed to cultures other than their own, and gained knowledge about systems of privilege and oppression (both racial and economic). Most of the time these experiences came about as part of the content of a course that asked them to work in groups with people whose ideas and backgrounds were different from their own. One student described the experience in this way: "I have gained inner confidence with discussion-based classes, empowered and confident to adapt to situations. Interaction with diverse classmates prepares and engages us in real world scenarios." Another stated, "My classes gave root to my awareness, and travelling on field study to take the Race in America class placed me in a civic engagement experience that gave me a deeper understanding of the democratic disparity people of color endured over time."

Several focus group participants also shared examples of classroom experiences in which they were challenged in some way—most frequently when instructors created situations where they had to think critically about an issue and work through problems with their classmates via dialogue or group activities. One student described the process: "[In] Bridging Community and Cultural Health my instructor really cared. She wanted us to learn more than she wanted us to do the work sheets. The entire class was about creating healthy communities, how to be engaged, and doing it ourselves. This was the most democratic approach to learning I have ever been involved in at school." Another added, "One class sticks out in my mind and that is American Radicalism. The teacher was excellent in helping to understand the concepts and perspectives. Our instructor facilitated discussion that allowed everyone equal time to say their piece and work through the conversations. I appreciate teachers who facilitate your learning and not just leave it up to me to teach myself."

As these statements make clear, MCTC students had no problems identifying the ways in which their college fulfills its civic mission. Furthermore, these civic experiences affect students' lives and learning in meaningful ways.

Student Views on the Workforce Mission of the College.   MCTC students also easily identified ways that the college fulfills its workforce mission. Their examples similarly fall into three categories: (a) teaching content and skills in the classroom, (b) experiential learning opportunities and mentoring, and (c) in-class opportunities to develop *soft* skills.

In discussions about the workforce mission of the college, students talked about the importance of teaching specific knowledge and skills, both discipline related (e.g., terms and practices related to human services) and more universal, such as writing and the use of technology. As one stated, "Positive instructors in my major give you real life examples to ready yourself for the workplace." Another related, "My classes make me feel as if I will be skillful with technology and studies that enhance the [discipline-related] skills that I'm learning."

Several students also shared examples of internships or experiences in their field that helped them develop their job skills. Further, they cited professional development opportunities offered by specific programs and more informal mentoring from peers and faculty as experiences that aided their efforts to successfully navigate their degree program and identify their passions and talents. Statements such as the following were common: "My internship at the sexual violence center has given me invaluable training. MCTC has these opportunities that should be made available to everyone." "I'm currently on internship near Minneapolis. The teacher stopped in to inquire about my well-being, pushing me to try new methods. It has built my confidence in my own abilities and gives the training to succeed."

Focus group participants also highlighted in-class experiences during which they had the opportunity to engage in discussions and group projects with individuals who have ideas different than their own. One related that her "Inter-Cultural Communication class explored global differences, and going into social work this will be useful. It gave me a learning experience that helps prepare me for real world interactions. My group project on Tibetans and Ethiopians gave me a global sense of social work. It helped me engage other cultures, making me more skillful." Another said, "My Reading teacher tells us you have to accept everyone's backgrounds. You don't have to agree but you must understand where they derive their point of view. Don't close your mind because you debilitate yourself then." A third student explained it this way: "My teachers give you the opportunity to learn how to figure it out on your own. They place you in diverse groups, letting you hear different ideas to help formulate answers that you may have never considered before."

One of the central questions posed by this project is how the civic and workforce missions of the college can be integrated in practice. The fact that group work, discussions on campus, and experiential learning experiences off campus (field trips, volunteer opportunities, internships) were highlighted when students were asked about both the civic and workforce missions suggests two things. First, there are areas on and off campus where this integration is already taking place, and second, the institution should be investing resources in these areas to more effectively pursue its civic and workforce goals and to scale up the types of activities that are already taking place. This last point is supported by student responses to the final question in each of the focus groups in which participants were asked to suggest ways that MCTC could more effectively pursue the two goals. There was a strong consensus in each group around the need for physical spaces where students could interact with and learn from one another, as well as the need for additional off-campus learning experiences, especially for students in liberal arts programs who do not have internship or service learning requirements as part of their degree requirements.

Faculty and Staff Views of MCTC's Civic and Workforce Missions

In addition to focus groups with students, I also conducted three less formal discussions with MCTC faculty and staff. The first was with social science faculty, and the remaining two were with a mix of faculty and staff attending employee development days. In those discussions, I asked the participants to share their perceptions of the civic and workforce mission of the college. In addition, I asked several follow-up questions tailored to the specific groups. These discussions, unlike the student focus groups, were not recorded and transcribed verbatim. However, detailed notes were taken during all three and the paragraphs that follow summarize the main themes covered in each.

During the first discussion, I asked 13 faculty from various social science departments two questions: 1) What connections can you make between the work that you do and the civic and workforce missions of the college? and 2) Regarding the efforts to develop a collegewide approach to internships and other types of community-based learning, what place do you see for the liberal arts in this discussion and what is your view of the relevance of this discussion to the work that we do in the social sciences?

The participants in this discussion focused strongly on the second question, during which concerns were raised about several issues, including (a) the logistical difficulties of setting up community-based learning opportunities for students and the type of support faculty would receive to pursue and implement such opportunities; (b) the development of field experiences that are appropriate for students at the college (first- and second-year college students, students with heavy family and work obligations, students challenged by basic skills such as writing); and (c) possible resistance to collegewide initiatives due to a perception among faculty that such initiatives are not given the institutional support to be carried out effectively.

The second discussion, which was facilitated by English faculty member Michael Kuhne and myself, was held with seven faculty members (all but one from liberal arts departments) and two students. The third, which I facilitated, involved two liberal arts faculty members and five staff members. During these discussions, participants were asked to share their perceptions about the extent to which the college fulfills its civic and workforce missions. These questions were asked in the context of a broader conversation about the role of higher education in society.

During these two facilitated discussions, several themes emerged. The first was a connection made by several liberal arts faculty and staff members between the workforce mission of the college and what they perceive as a growing emphasis on workforce development at the college, at the expense of the college's civic mission. Several faculty participants in the second group described a discourse about higher education among legislators at the state capitol, which they viewed as being devoid of any references to preparing citizens and that emphasized the production of workers at the lowest cost. Participants in both groups also shared their perception that the college leadership primarily focused on building community partnerships with private corporations, linking the pursuit of such relationships to dwindling public support for higher education. Faculty and staff who noted these trends also expressed concerns about what they saw as the diminishing support of and respect for liberal arts education among policymakers, college leaders, and society as a whole.

A second theme that emerged was the contradiction that some faculty members saw between the workforce and civic missions of the college. Those who expressed this perspective were from liberal arts departments and primarily viewed the workforce mission of the college as being pursued through occupational training that prepared students to adapt to existing systems (e.g., capitalism and the inequities it produces). In contrast, they associated the civic mission with liberal arts education that encouraged students to think critically and challenge unjust systems.

The third theme centered around ways to challenge the perception that the civic mission of the college needed to be pursued outside of the college. Several participants suggested that the college could focus on its civic mission by doing more to embody democracy in its practices in the classroom, within and between in departments, and in its overall governance. Several participants also challenged the notion that helping "the community"— which is often associated with the civic mission of the college—necessarily means working off campus. Those who made this point cited how many of our own students are experiencing homelessness and that efforts to address community issues such as this could focus on needs right on campus.

Challenges and Possibilities for Integrating Workforce and Civic Missions

After conducting student focus groups and facilitated discussions with faculty and staff, two somewhat contradictory things became clear. On one hand, faculty and staff may not always be aware of how the civic and workforce missions can be integrated, may be wary of doing so given a perception that the civic function will lose out to the workforce mission, and may worry that the institution cannot or will not provide adequate support for the types of experiences and activities that can facilitate a connection between the two. On the other hand, students perceive the ways in which MCTC pursues its civic and workforce missions in much the same ways: primarily through structured off-campus experiences, as well as group work and intense classroom discussions on topics of interest to them and the community. What's more, students want more of all of these experiences. Given these major takeaways, what can community colleges do to more thoroughly integrate their civic and workforce missions? The paragraphs that follow identify some possible approaches.

Include Students as Central Actors in the Discussion.   Student focus groups revealed that students with a wide range of educational and career goals appreciate learning experiences that provide opportunities to engage in the world outside of the classroom, learn course content in an experiential manner, and develop practical skills. What is also clear is that the divide between workforce and civic missions of the college exists to a much lesser extent in the minds of students than in the minds of faculty and staff. One of the questions I had at the start of this project was whether or not students in liberal arts programs would have more to share about how the civic mission of the college was reflected in their experiences and the CTE students more to share about the workforce mission. This was not the case. Students in liberal arts programs—even those who were on the general education/transfer track and unsure what career path they would like to pursue—had clear perceptions about how their experiences were or were not preparing them with the skills they thought they needed for the workplace. In addition, students from CTE programs often were more able to quickly articulate the connections between the workforce *and* civic missions and their experiences inside and outside of the classroom. The fact that these missions are largely about the experiences we create for students, as well as the fact that students are less likely than faculty to carry baggage about liberal versus career and technical education, point to the need for students to be centrally involved in these discussions.

Create Strategic Alliances and Collaborative Spaces to Overcome Institutional Barriers and Academic Silos.   In 2013, I was involved in the *MCTCWorks!* program, an initiative that attempted to develop a collegewide approach to internships and other types of community-based learning. This initiative, which was led by associate vice president of workforce development Mike Christenson, was sparked by the recognized need for more institutional support for field-based experiences, as well as by evidence suggesting that students who gain experience working in their field of study have higher retention rates, higher graduation rates, more success as far as job placements in their field of study, and higher wages once they graduate (National Association of Colleges and Employers, 2013). Although the majority of the faculty members in the *MCTCWorks!* working group were from CTE programs, several liberal arts faculty, such as myself, were also invited to participate. The proposal produced by this committee included several components, such as academically aligned work–study, the creation of a student work cooperative, and enhanced support for internships and other community-based learning opportunities for students.

The challenges faced while implementing this initiative illustrate the barriers that exist at many institutions to practically integrating the civic and workforce missions of community colleges. One of those barriers is rooted in the ways that activities associated with the civic and workforce missions are funded. Attempts to foster collaboration between liberal arts and CTE programs through formal institutional channels were restricted due to rules attached to the funding that colleges receive. For example, the two staff members who are paid to work on the *MCTCWorks!* project are supported by federal Perkins funds, which restrict them from officially working with programs that are not career or technical in nature. The lack of resources for liberal arts faculty and students to take part in opportunities such as those proposed by the *MCTCWorks!* task force has become more dire with the absence of general fund money to support this work and administrative decisions not to fill service learning and career services support positions.

One approach to addressing this problem is exemplified by MCTC's community development associate of science program. This program, founded in 2010, prepares students for a wide range of careers in nonprofit organizations, community development corporations, government, and the private sector, all of which aim to bring about community change. Although the program is housed in liberal arts, it has an advisory committee composed of individuals from nonprofit organizations, community development corporations, government, and bachelor's degree granting institutions, and incorporates courses and field-based learning experiences with learning goals typically recognized as job skills.

This program has been building strategic alliances with nonprofit organizations, and these have enabled it to pursue its goals without support from the college's general fund. For example, Community Learning Partnership (CLP)—a national network of community change studies programs with a mission of developing a workforce of community change agents—has supported four to eight credits of release time for a faculty member to coordinate MCTC's program since fall 2011. In addition, the Native American Community Development Institute, in partnership with CLP and program faculty, has raised funds to provide stipends to community development students while they are fulfilling their internship requirement.

A second barrier stems from the divergent historical origins of liberal arts and career and technical education, and the challenges that can arise when community and technical colleges are forged out of separate institutions united under a common mission and vision. The divides that remain, even after existing as a single institution for many years, can lead to a lack of communication between the liberal arts and CTE departments, as well as assumptions about what colleagues on the other side of the divide are doing. During the faculty discussions, I found that many of the liberal arts professors who took part in this study tended to identify more with the civic mission of the college and associate the workforce mission with CTE departments. Some also associated the workforce mission with institutional and societal trends that are leading to the devaluing of liberal education. On the other hand, although many CTE faculty and staff place high importance on training students to understand and engage the communities where they work, some feel excluded from the dominant discourse in academia about the civic mission of higher education, which is sometimes seen as narrowly focused on political activism.

A way to address these challenges is to create spaces where CTE and liberal arts faculty can share ideas, learn from one another, and challenge the assumptions that sometimes emerge on either side of the liberal arts/CTE divide. As a liberal arts faculty member with a long-time interest in civic engagement, I found that one of the most rewarding aspects of this project was having the opportunity to learn about the innovative collaborative work that my CTE colleagues are doing with each other and with community organizations. In the process, I also had the opportunity to share my own work building the community development program's pre-internship and internship programs and the ways that I adapted models drawn from liberal arts-based internship literature with the practices of our CTE departments.

Just as I believe that individual institutions would benefit from the creation of such spaces, I also believe that national dialogues about the civic and workforce missions of community colleges would benefit from them as well. Too often, liberal arts and CTE faculty discuss these issues in isolation from one another and without the insights of students. Deepening the discussion about the role of higher education in making democracy work in the 21st century necessitates widening the actors involved and challenging the structures that discourage the transgression of these boundaries.

Reference

National Association of Colleges and Employers. (2013). *Class of 2013: Paid interns outpace unpaid peers on job offers, salaries.* Washington, DC: Author.

LENA JONES *is professor of political science at Minneapolis Community and Technical College.*

INDEX

NEW DIRECTIONS FOR COMMUNITY COLLEGE
ORDER FORM SUBSCRIPTION AND SINGLE ISSUES

DISCOUNTED BACK ISSUES:

Use this form to receive 20% off all back issues of *New Directions for Community College*.
All single issues priced at **$23.20** (normally $29.00)

TITLE	ISSUE NO.	ISBN

Call 1-800-835-6770 or see mailing instructions below. When calling, mention the promotional code JBNND to receive your discount. For a complete list of issues, please visit www.wiley.com/WileyCDA/WileyTitle/productCd-CC.html

SUBSCRIPTIONS: (1 YEAR, 4 ISSUES)

☐ New Order   ☐ Renewal

U.S.	☐ Individual: $89	☐ Institutional: $356
CANADA/MEXICO	☐ Individual: $89	☐ Institutional: $398
ALL OTHERS	☐ Individual: $113	☐ Institutional: $434

Call 1-800-835-6770 or see mailing and pricing instructions below.
Online subscriptions are available at www.onlinelibrary.wiley.com

ORDER TOTALS:

Issue / Subscription Amount: $ _____

Shipping Amount: $ _____
(for single issues only – subscription prices include shipping)

Total Amount: $ _____

SHIPPING CHARGES:

First Item	$6.00
Each Add'l Item	$2.00

(No sales tax for U.S. subscriptions. Canadian residents, add GST for subscription orders. Individual rate subscriptions must be paid by personal check or credit card. Individual rate subscriptions may not be resold as library copies.)

BILLING & SHIPPING INFORMATION:

☐ **PAYMENT ENCLOSED:** *(U.S. check or money order only. All payments must be in U.S. dollars.)*

☐ **CREDIT CARD:**   ☐ VISA   ☐ MC   ☐ AMEX

Card number _____Exp. Date_____

Card Holder Name_____Card Issue # _____

Signature _____Day Phone_____

☐ **BILL ME:** *(U.S. institutional orders only. Purchase order required.)*

Purchase order # _____
Federal Tax ID 13559302 • GST 89102-8052

Name_____

Address_____

Phone_____ E-mail_____

Copy or detach page and send to: **John Wiley & Sons, Inc. / Jossey Bass**
PO Box 55381
Boston, MA 02205-9850

PROMO JBNND

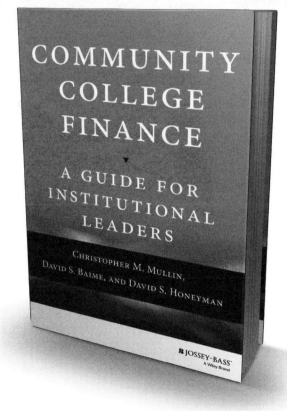

WITHDRAWAL